The Sutra of Explaining the Profound Secret

(Samdhinirmocana Sutra)

An English Version of the Chinese
Jie Shen Mi Jing Rendered from Sanskrit
by Master Xuanzang

Translated by

Naichen Chen

Published by Wheatmark®
2030 East Speedway Boulevard, Suite 106
Tucson, Arizona 85719 USA
www.wheatmark.com

ISBN: 979-8-88747-027-6
ISBN: 979-8-88747-028-3
LCCN: 2022920106

Bulk ordering discounts are available through Wheatmark, Inc. For more information, email orders@wheatmark.com or call 1-888-934-0888.

Contents

Preface:
The Causes and Conditions of the Assembly

This is what I heard.

There was a time the Bhagavat lived in the most superior and brightest dignity of seven treasures, and emitted great, brilliant lights to shine all over the boundless worlds in innumerable directions. This was an infinite space, beautifully laid out with exquisite decorations. Its circumference was immeasurably broad that even went far beyond the three realms.

Where the Buddha went, all appeared superior to the mundane world. His virtuous roots would arise with extreme self-ease. His consciousness was always with pure form. Wherever the Thus-Comer stayed, the great bodhisattvas would gather together and surrounded him, along with numberless heavenly deities, nagas, yaksas, gandharvas, asuras, garudas, kimnaras, mahoragas, humans, and nonhumans. He embraced the widely expanding delight of dharma taste and was dedicated to bringing justice and benefits to all sentient beings so as to remove their various vexations, disasters, and bondages of defilements, and let them stay far away from evil demons.

The magnificent dignity of the Thus-Comer was superior to all kinds of splendid solemnity. The Thus-Comer's path was great mindfulness and wise actions; his vehicle was great concentration and exquisite contemplation; and his gate was great emptiness, formlessness, and nonaspiration. His palace was built by the followers of King Great Jewel Flowers, but was beautified and glorified by innumerable merits and virtues.

The Bhagavat had achieved the purest enlightenment featured with nondualistic and formless phenomena of the dharmas. He dwelled where the Buddhas stayed, in which the equality of the Buddha nature was attained without hindrance. His changeless ultimate truth spread with no obstacles. What he achieved and established was inconceivable.

Passing through the equal dharma nature of the three phases of time, the Bhagavat's body flowed all over the worlds. He knew all dharmas without skepticism and hesitation, accomplished great enlightenment in all actions, and understood various dharma paths without doubt and perplexity. His body could not be perceived when he appeared. He owned the perfect knowledge that all bodhisattvas were still looking for. Once the bodhisattvas could acquire the nondualistic wisdom in which the Buddhas stayed, they would be able to dwell in the superior other shore, where the Thus-Comer's exquisite knowledge of liberation was so pure that no defilement was involved. They then would also realize the Thus-Comer's exquisite knowledge transcending the differentiation between the middle and extreme ways. Nothing else in dharma realm would be superior to the Buddha's state of equality expanding as far as to the end of empty space and into the infinite future.

There were innumerable great voice-hearers present beside the Thus-Comer. They were well tamed and stayed in comfort and harmony; all were the Buddha's sons and daughters. Their minds were well liberated, and their wisdom was well released. They observed pure precept and enjoyed the dharma. They had heard and learned a lot, and what they heard and learned were well retained and accumulated. They could reflect well on what they intended to think, speak well what they intended to say, and do well what they intended to do. They had remarkably achieved rapid wisdom, quick understanding, sharp judgment, appropriate expression, intelligent decision making, great wisdom, broad wisdom, and unequaled equal wisdom. They had realized the threefold knowledge in wisdom gem, so they could remember their previous lives, had successfully developed supernatural eyes, and extinguished all flaws. They had experienced the uppermost joy of dharma presently and dwelled in the great pure field of bliss, and both their demeanor and inner tranquility were perfectly fulfilled. They had obtained superior patience and tenderness in heart without diminution. That was because they had followed and practiced the Buddha's noble teachings so well.

There were also innumerable bodhisattvas from different Buddha lands present in the assembly. They all had stayed in great vehicle and followed the great-vehicle path. They treated all sentient beings equally, and stayed away from the discrimination between differentiation and nondifferentiation. They had subjugated and destroyed all demons and adversaries and refrained from pursuing the paths of voice-hearer and self-enlightened one. Overwhelmed by the broad and great joy of dharma, they conquered the five kinds of fears, entered the stage of nonregression, and ceased the suffering and vexations that all sentient beings had encountered. The leading ones among the bodhisattvas present in the assembly were Understanding

Profound Secret Meaning Great Bodhisattva, Asking Reasonably Great Bodhisattva, Dharma Flowing Great Bodhisattva, Virtuous Pure Wisdom Great Bodhisattva, Broad Wisdom Great Bodhisattva, Virtue Base Great Bodhisattva, Ultimate Meaning Arising Great Bodhisattva, Viewing in Freedom Great Bodhisattva, Maitreya Great Bodhisattva, and Manjusri Great Bodhisattva.

The Forms of the Ultimate Meaning

At that time, Asking Reasonably Great Bodhisattva asked Understanding Profound Secret Meaning Great Bodhisattva in front of the Buddha, "The most superior one, it is said that all dharmas are nondualistic. What are all dharmas? Why are they nondualistic?"

Understanding Profound Secret Meaning Bodhisattva replied, "Good gentleman, all dharmas can be briefly divided into two kinds: the conditioned and the unconditioned. The conditioned dharmas are neither conditioned nor unconditioned, and the unconditioned dharmas are neither unconditioned nor conditioned."

Asking Reasonably Bodhisattva asked again, "The most superior one, why are the conditioned dharmas neither conditioned nor unconditioned, and the unconditioned dharmas neither unconditioned nor conditioned?"

Understanding Profound Secret Meaning Bodhisattva replied, "The conditioned dharmas are so named because they are expressed by the language established by the Buddha. The established language is created in terms of universal attachment. As we look deeply into it, we will see that the language spoken in terms of universal attachment is not real. Such an understanding turns out to be based on the unconditioned rather than the conditioned perspective. Good gentleman, when people say that something is unconditioned, they will fall in the category of language and concept. Even when trying to stay away from the differentiation between the conditioned and the unconditioned dharmas without saying much, they are still in the category of language and concept. But the holy ones do not speak without reason; they do this because of an important thing. The holy ones realize and attain the perfect and universal enlightenment when they become free from relying on language and concept through developing perfect knowledge and views. After that, they undertake an important task: teaching the sentient beings to let them get rid of the attachment to the names and words of the dharmas, so they will attain the perfect and universal enlightenment. It is with such an attempt that the holy ones have expediently established the provisional names and forms, the so-called conditioned dharmas.

"Good gentleman, the unconditioned dharma is also a provisional name established by the Buddha. The language is created in terms of universal attachment, so it is not real in the final analysis; it is thus not an unconditioned dharma.

"Good gentleman, to speak about the conditioned dharma will fall in the category of language and concept. Even if we do not say much intending to avoid the two extremes between the conditioned and the unconditioned dharmas, we are still in the category of language and concept. The holy ones have not taught this for nothing. They have attained the perfect and universal enlightenment because they have gotten rid of the bondage of language and concept by means of developing perfect knowledge and views. They further teach the sentient beings not to be attached to the language, so as to let them also realize and attain the perfect and universal enlightenment. That is why the holy ones establish the name of the unconditioned for the dharma nature that is in actuality apart from the language."

At that time, Asking Reasonably Bodhisattva asked Understanding Profound Secret Meaning Bodhisattva again, "Most superior one, the holy ones have attained the perfect and universal enlightenment by means of developing the perfect knowledge and views apart from the names and languages. They have further established the names and concepts for the conditioned and unconditioned dharmas in order to guide the sentient beings to become liberated from the attachment to the language and concepts of the dharmas, and also attain the perfect and universal enlightenment. Why do the holy ones do this?"

Understanding Profound Secret Meaning Bodhisattva replied, "Good gentleman, a magician or his or her disciple piled up grass, leaves, rocks, and rubble debris at a four-way intersection and played tricks with them to make transformed elephants, horses, carts, walking people, gems, pearls, crystals, shells, jades, corals, and rice and cereals in storehouses. Ignorant people would be attached to what they saw and heard, insisting that these transformed matters were real and those who disagreed with them were foolish and deluded. These were the people who needed to practice more contemplations and investigations.

"Some sentient beings were not foolish; rather, they were wise enough to tell the real from the illusory. They realized that these elephants, horses, carts, walking people, jewelry, pearls, crystals, shells, jades, corals, and rice and cereals were transformed from grass, leaves, rocks, and rubble debris. They were also aware that as ones were deluded, they would mistake the illusory for real. They thus came to the conclusion that the phenomena appearing before our eyes were not real; they were not as what we saw and heard. In order to correct the erroneous views, they would speak out the reality that they discovered. These were the ones who needed no more contemplations and investigations.

"Some sentient beings were ignorant, the so-called ordinary sentient beings. They had not attained the transcendental wisdom possessed by the holy ones, so they could not realize that the dharma natures were apart from the language. They did not really know the conditioned dharmas and the unconditioned dharmas, and mistook the illusions that they had seen and heard for real and insisted that they were correct and others were wrong. These sentient beings should do more contemplations and investigations.

"Some sentient beings were not ignorant. They had seen the noble truth and attained the transcendental wisdom possessed by the holy ones. They realized that all dharma natures were apart from the language and concepts. When hearing about the conditioned and the unconditioned dharmas, they would think, 'The conditioned and the unconditioned dharmas are not really existent. They are caused by differentiation. They are like the illusions that confuse people and make them go astray from the wisdom of enlightenment and initiate differentiation between the conditioned and the unconditioned dharmas. The truth is not what we see or hear. With this insight, we must stay with what we really know.' In order to express the correct understanding, they would claim this truth. These sentient beings needed no more contemplations and investigations. Good gentlemen, the holy ones are able to attain the perfect and universal enlightenment because they have gotten rid of the language and concepts owing to their perfect knowledge and views. In order to let other sentient beings also attain the perfect and universal enlightenment, the holy ones have created provisional names and forms, and established the conditioned dharmas and the unconditioned dharmas."

At that time, Understanding Profound Secret Meaning Bodhisattva reiterated this meaning in verse:

The Buddha says there is no dualistic meaning apart from
  language.
The fathomless meaning is not the path the ignorant ones
  practice.
The foolish ones are puzzled out of ignorance.
They are attached to dualism and argue nonsensically.
They are either restless or without correct concentration and
Will drift in birth and death and suffer for a long time.
As arguing in conflict with correct knowledge,
They will be reborn as oxen, sheep, and so forth.

At that time, Dharma Flowing Great Bodhisattva said to the Buddha, "World-Honored One, passing as many worlds as the sands of seventy-two Ganges from this land in the east, there is a world named Possessing Great Name, and the Thus-Comer in that land is named Vast Great Name. I just came from there a few days ago. I once saw in that world a group of seventy-seven thousand devoted other-path practitioners. They sat together with their master teacher to reflect on the characteristics of ultimate truth. They discussed, measured, contemplated, investigated, and sought and could not successfully obtain the ultimate meaning of the truth. However, they did figure out many ideas. Some ideas were transformed from others, while some were the variations of the similar interpretations. But these ideas were all in contradiction. These practitioners argued against each other, criticized each other, and became very upset. At last, they had to leave the assembly. World-Honored One, at that time I thought that the Thus-Comer's birth in this world is such a wonderful and unique event. Because of his birth, we are privileged to access the ultimate truth. The ultimate meaning that the Thus-Comer teaches goes beyond all kinds of reflection and can be realized and understood thoroughly."

After hearing these words, the World-Honored One said to Dharma Flowing Bodhisattva, "It is as you say, good gentleman. I attained the perfect and universal enlightenment because of realizing the ultimate truth that is superior to and beyond human thinking and imagination. After the attainment of the perfect and universal enlightenment, I have lectured on, demonstrated, and explained it through all kinds of establishment in order to illumine others. Why? As I said before, the ultimate meaning is the truth verified and realized by the holy ones from within, while reflection and investigation are the ways adopted by ordinary sentient beings through reasoning. Therefore, Dharma Flowing, you will see that because of this difference, the ultimate meaning is superior to the level of investigation and reflection.

"Furthermore, Dharma Flowing, I will say that the ultimate meaning is formless while reflection and investigation rely on form. Dharma Flowing, because of this reason, the ultimate meaning surpasses investigation and reflection. Furthermore, Dharma Flowing, I will also say that the ultimate meaning is unspeakable, while investigation and reflection rely on speech. Dharma Flowing, because of this reason, the ultimate meaning is superior to investigation and reflection.

"Furthermore, Dharma Flowing, I will say that the ultimate meaning is completely free from representation, while investigation and reflection need representation to keep them going. Therefore, Dharma Flowing, you must know that the ultimate meaning is superior to investigation and reflection. Furthermore, Dharma Flowing, the ultimate meaning does not invite controversial arguments, while investigation and reflection always get involved in controversial arguments. Therefore, Dharma Flowing, you must see that the ultimate meaning is superior to investigation and reflection.

"Dharma Flowing, you must know that some people are only used to the taste of spice and bitterness for the rest of their lives. I do not think that they can figure out, measure, believe, or understand what the tastes of honey, crystal sugar, and other delicious food are really like.

"Because the people are used to the burning fire of desires caused by greed for a long time, they are unable to figure out, measure, believe, or really understand the inner exquisite pleasures of getting far away caused by the extinction of the senses produced by sight, sound, smell, taste, and touch.

"Because they have been fond of and attached to speaking nonsensical filthy words for a long time, they will not be able to figure out, measure, believe, or understand the joy of inner quietude and tranquility.

"Because they have been fond of and attached to the perceived knowledge and conceptual images for a long time, they will not be able to figure out, measure, believe, or understand how ones really feel when they are permanently free from the incorrect view of selfness and stay in ultimate nirvana.

"Dharma Flowing, you must know that because some people have been attached to and fond of the controversial arguments about the selfness and the associated images for a long time, they will not be able to figure out, measure, believe, or understand how the people of the continent of Uttarakuru really feel when they are free from the controversial arguments about the selfness and the associated images. Therefore, Dharma Flowing, to rely on thinking will not allow one to figure out, measure, believe, or understand the ultimate meaning that transcends all forms of thinking."

At that time, the World-Honored One reiterated this meaning in verse:

The realization from within is free from the forms.
It is beyond speech and other representations.
The ultimate truth will cease all controversial arguments
And transcend the forms of investigation and reflection.

At that time, Virtuous Pure Wisdom Great Bodhisattva said to the Buddha, "World-Honored One, it is very unique and unusual! It is wonderful that you can give such exquisite teachings. World-Honored One's teachings about the characteristics of the ultimate meanings of the truth are very subtle and profound. They surpass the sameness and differences of the natures and features of all dharmas and are very difficult to thoroughly understand.

"World-Honored One, I once saw a crowd of bodhisattvas who were in the process of reaching the stage of definitive superior understandings and practices. They sat together and discussed the sameness and differences between the ultimate meanings of the truth and the mental images of the perceived knowledge.

"In this meeting, one group of bodhisattvas contended that the forms of the ultimate truth were not different from the mental images. Another group argued that the ultimate truth was not totally the same as the mental images; that is, they were different. Some other bodhisattvas were puzzled and had such questions in their minds: Who was telling the truth and who was not? Who acted in accord with the truth and who did not? They were confused because some bodhisattvas had claimed that the forms of the ultimate truth were not different from the mental images, while others said that they were not the same.

"World-Honored One, as I witnessed this, I thought to myself that all these good gentlemen were really ignorant and stubborn. They were not bright and smart, and did not act following the path of truth. They did not understand that the ultimate truth is subtle and fathomless; it transcends the sameness and differences of the natures and forms."

After hearing these words, the World-Honored One said to Virtuous Pure Wisdom Great Bodhisattva, "Good gentleman, what you say is quite right. Some people are so ignorant and stubborn that they neither understand the truth nor follow the correct path. They do not understand the subtle and profound meaning of the ultimate truth. They do not know that the ultimate truth is superior to and exceeds the perceived knowledge that is featured with the distinction between sameness and difference. Why? Virtuous Pure Wisdom Bodhisattva, as ones are constrained by the narrow definition of the perceived knowledge of the world, they will not be able to thoroughly understand the forms of the ultimate truth, nor realize insightfully the ultimate truth.

"Why? Virtuous Pure Wisdom! If the ultimate truth were the same as the perceived images, then all ordinary sentient beings should have presently seen the truth, attained the unsurpassed expediency, peace, stability, and nirvana; or have realized insightfully anuttara-samyak-saṃbodhi.

"If the ultimate truth were always different from the perceived knowledge, then the ones who have seen the ultimate truth would not necessarily cast off the perceived images, and thus would not be relieved from the bondage of the forms. If they were not relieved from the bondage of the forms, they would not be relieved from the bondage of heavy vexations either. Since they were not relieved from these two kinds of bondage, ones who have already seen the ultimate truth should not have attained the unsurpassed expediency, peace, stability, and nirvana or realized insightfully anuttara-samyak-saṃbodhi.

"Virtuous Pure Wisdom, not all ordinary sentient beings have seen the ultimate truth presently, nor have they attained the unsurpassed expediency, peace, stability, and nirvana or anuttara-samyak-saṃbodhi. Therefore, it does not make sense to say that the ultimate truth and the perceived knowledge are the same. Those who make such an assertion do not act in accord with the correct path of the truth.

"Virtuous Pure Wisdom, those who have not seen the ultimate truth and thus cannot cast off the mental images will see the ultimate truth and cast off the mental images someday in the future; those who have not gotten rid of the bondage of the forms will get rid of the forms someday in the future; and those who have not been relieved from the heavy bondage of vexations will be relieved from the heavy bondage of vexations someday in the future. When the sentient beings are liberated from these two bondages, they will attain the unsurpassed expediency, peace, stability, and nirvana or the perfect and universal bodhi. Therefore, it is evident that the ultimate truth and the perceived images are not always different. Those who say that the ultimate truth and the perceived images are always different are unreasonable and do not act in accord with the correct path of the truth.

"Furthermore, Virtuous Pure Wisdom, if the ultimate truth were the same as the perceived knowledge, then as the mental images fall in contaminated forms, the ultimate truth would also fall in contaminated forms. Virtuous Pure Wisdom, if the ultimate truth and the perceived knowledge were always different, then they would not share the same characteristics. Virtuous Pure Wisdom, because the ultimate truth would not fall in contaminated forms, and the perceived knowledge also shares some common traits with the ultimate truth, it is unreasonable to say that they are the same or they are always different. It is based on this reason to say that such assertions are contrary to the truth.

"Furthermore, Virtuous Pure Wisdom, if the ultimate truth and the perceived knowledge were totally not different, then all mental images would not be different from the ultimate truth. If this is the case, then the practitioners of contemplation would only need to see what they have seen, hear what they have heard, awake to what they have awoken to, and know what they have known and would not need to seek the ultimate truth.

"If the ultimate truth were always different from the perceived knowledge, then we would not say that all phenomena are without selfness and the manifestation of the selflessness of all dharmas is the ultimate truth. Besides, if this is the case, the different manifestations of the contaminated and pure forms of the same dharma would occur concurrently.

"Virtuous Pure Wisdom, because the mental images of the perceived knowledge appear as different from the ultimate truth, the contemplation practitioners will not just see what they have seen, hear what they have heard, awake to what they have awoken to, and know what they have known; they need to further pursue the ultimate truth. Because the selflessness of the perceived dharmas are also named the ultimate truth and the different manifestations of the pure and the contaminated dharmas do not occur concurrently, it does not make sense to say that the ultimate truth and the perceived knowledge are totally the same or are always different. If we insist to say so, we are not in accord with the correct path of the truth.

"Virtuous Pure Wisdom, it is difficult to say that the white color of a shell is the same as or different from the shell itself. So is the relationship between the golden color of the gold and the gold itself. It is also like the wonderful music played by a stringed harp and the harp itself. They are the same and they are different as well. Again, it is difficult to say that the aroma of agaru incense and the agaru incense itself are the same or different; the strong spicy flavor of pepper and the pepper itself are the same or different; the softness of cotton and the cotton itself are the same or different; and the delicious taste of ghee and the ghee itself are the same or different. It is difficult to imagine that the impermanence of the dharmas and the dharmas themselves are the same or different; the suffering of the sentient beings caused by the flaws and the flaws themselves are the same or different; the selfless nature of individual human beings and the human beings themselves are the same or different; and the manifestations of turbulence and impurity in greed and the greed itself are the same or different. So are the instances of hatred and ignorance.

"Therefore, Virtuous Pure Wisdom, we cannot say that the ultimate truth is totally the same as the perceived knowledge or they are always different. Virtuous Pure Wisdom, I attained the perfect and universal enlightenment because I have realized insightfully the ultimate truth that is subtle and very subtle, profound and very profound, and difficult and very difficult to understand; it transcends the sameness and differences of the natures and the forms of all dharmas. After my enlightenment, I have taught sentient beings this meaning of the ultimate truth, illumining them by demonstrating, explaining, and establishing the ultimate meaning of the truth."

At that time, the World-Honored One reiterated the same meaning in verse:

The ultimate meaning of the phenomena of all dharmas
Goes beyond the sameness and differences of the natures and
  forms.
Trying to differentiate between their sameness and differences
Is not in accord with the correct path of the truth.

The ordinary sentient beings are bound up in the forms,
They will also be bound up in the heavy bondage of vexations.
It is crucial to diligently cultivate concentration and contem-
 plation,
So they will be able to attain liberation.

At that time, the World-Honored One asked the senior bhiksu Well Appearing One [Subhuti], "Well Appearing One, how many sentient beings are besieged by arrogance to overstate their achievements and commend what they have understood? How many sentient beings have stayed away from arrogance and commend what they have understood?"

The senior bhiksu Well Appearing One replied to the Buddha, "World-Honored One, as I know, very few sentient beings are not arrogant and know accurately their own achievements, but numberless sentient beings are self-conceited to overstate their achievements. They are overwhelmed by arrogance and commend what they have understood.

"World-Honored One, I once lived in a silent retreat located in a large forest, where I saw a lot of bhiksus nearby. They gathered together in different groups after the sunset and talked about various topics. They expressed their own opinions based on what they had attained in their contemplations and commended what they had understood.

"Some bhiksus were interested in the category of the aggregates. Because they had gained some insightful understandings of the phenomena of aggregates, the arising of the aggregates, the exhaustion of the aggregates, the extinction of the aggregates, and the realization of the extinction of the aggregates, they commended what they had understood.

"So did the bhiksus who were interested in the category of the spheres or the category of dependent origination. Those interested in the category of the food also had gained some insightful understandings of the characteristics of the food and the arising, exhaustion, extinction, and the realization of the extinction of the food, so they expressed their own opinions and commended what they had understood.

"Some bhiksus had attained the meanings of the noble truths, the forms of the truths, the universal knowledge of the truths, the permanent cessation of suffering, and the realization of the truths as well as their cultivation. These bhiksus thus commended what they had understood.

"Another category was that of the realm. These bhiksus had grasped the meanings of the realm, including the forms, various traits, more than one nature, the extinction of the realm, as well as the realization of the extinction of the realm. These bhiksus thus commended what they had understood.

"Another category was that of the mindfulness. The bhiksus of this group focused on the correct mindfulness. They had grasped its forms, the subject and the objects, the cultivation, and the effort in making positive things that had not yet happened happen and making existing positive things grow and expand. They thus commended what they had understood.

"Like the bhiksus who focused on the mindfulness, so did the ones who focused on the four correct endeavors, the four bases of power, the five roots, the five powers, or the seven factors for enlightenment. There was also a group of bhiksus who would focus on the noble eightfold path; they had grasped its forms, the subjects, the objects, the cultivation, and the ways of making the eightfold path that had not yet happened happen and making the existing eightfold path grow and expand. These bhiksus thus contended what they had understood.

"World-Honored One, after seeing all of them, I had a thought in my mind: All these senior bhiksus had expressed their thoughts restricted in a facet of the forms of the dharmas in contemplation. They had all embraced a serious self-conceit overstating their own achievements and could not realize the universal taste and form of the superior ultimate meaning.

"World-Honored One, you are so unique! You always give teachings wonderfully! You teach us the characteristics of the ultimate truth, and say that it is subtle, subtlest; profound, most profound; and difficult, most difficult to understand thoroughly. You also say that the ultimate truth permeates all dharmas with one taste and one form. World-Honored One, these bhiksus have cultivated diligently, but still cannot understand the ultimate truth and its universal taste, not to mention the other-path practitioners."

At that time, the World-Honored One said to the senior monastic Well Appearing One, "Yes, it is as you say. I attained the perfect and universal enlightenment when I awakened to the meaning of the ultimate truth that is subtle and subtlest, profound and most profound, and difficult and most difficult to understand; it permeates all dharmas with one taste and one form. After attaining the enlightenment, I started to teach, demonstrate, and explain it to others, trying my best to make them understand. Why? Well Appearing One, I have demonstrated the ultimate truth that the effects caused by the aggregates are pure; the effects caused by the spheres, dependent origination, food, noble truths, realms, bases of mindfulness, correct endeavors, bases of power, roots, powers, factors for enlightenment, and the noble path are pure. All these effects are with one taste and one form. Therefore, Well Appearing One, you must know that the ultimate truth permeates all dharmas with one taste and one form.

"Furthermore, Well Appearing One, once the bhiksus have cultivated contemplation and thoroughly understand the selflessness of the realness of one single aggregate, they will not need to seek the selflessness of the realness of the rest of the aggregates, spheres, dependent origination, food, truths, realms, bases of mindfulness, correct endeavors, bases of power, roots, powers, factors for enlightenment, and noble path. If they follow this nondualistic ultimate meaning of realness to contemplate carefully, they will get to know how the ultimate truth permeates all dharmas with one taste and one form.

"Furthermore, Well Appearing One, if the ultimate meaning of the selfless nature of the realness of all dharmas had various different forms manifested by aggregates, food, truths, mindfulness, correct endeavors, bases of power, roots, powers, factors for enlightenment, and noble path, then the selfless nature of the realness of all dharmas should have been produced by some causes. If it were produced by causes, it would be the conditioned dharma. If it were the conditioned dharma, it would not be the ultimate meaning. If it were not the ultimate meaning, then we need to seek the ultimate meaning elsewhere. But the selfless nature of the realness of the dharmas does not arise based on cause and condition, nor is it the conditioned dharma, so it should be the ultimate truth. We do not need to seek the ultimate meaning elsewhere.

"Whether the Thus-Comer appears in the world or not, the dharma nature has always been well established, and the dharma realm has always dwelled peacefully. Therefore, Well Appearing One, you must know that the ultimate truth is universal and with only one taste and one form. Well Appearing One, like the formless empty space that permeates all different dharmas and does not differentiate and change but with only one taste and one form, so the ultimate meaning of the truth also permeates all dharmas with only one taste and one form."

At that time, the World-Honored One reiterated the same meaning in verse:

This universal form with one unified taste is
The ultimate meaning that all the Buddhas teach.
Those trying to differentiate among all dharmas
Should be the foolish and arrogant ones.

The Forms of the Mind Consciousness

At that time, Broad Wisdom Great Bodhisattva asked the Buddha, "World-Honored One, you once taught about the bodhisattvas as they are with secret skillfulness of mind consciousness. What are the bodhisattvas with secret skillfulness of mind consciousness? Why are they so established?"

After hearing what Broad Wisdom Great Bodhisattva said, the World-Honored One replied, "Excellent! Excellent! Broad Wisdom, you finally ask me such a profound question. I know you are asking in order to bring benefits and happiness to innumerable sentient beings. You are asking this question because you have great compassion over the heavenly beings, human beings, asuras, and so forth. You are with an attempt to bring justice, benefits, peace, and happiness to all of them. Now please listen to me carefully, I am going to talk about the secret meaning of the mind consciousness.

"Broad Wisdom, you must know that the sentient beings have reincarnated in birth and death in the six destinies. They are reborn in physical bodies through eggs, womb, or moisture; or they are just brought into existence through transformation. At the beginning of the birth process, the seeds comprised in mind consciousness mature. These seeds reorganize again and again, and then grow and expand based on two things that are ready to receive and hold them. One is the material sense roots with their functions, and the other is the forms and names created for perception, differentiation, speech, nonsensical arguments, and disposition. In the realm of form, these two things are present, while in the realm of formlessness, both are absent.

"Broad Wisdom, this consciousness is also named adana consciousness. Why? It is because this consciousness always follows the physical body and is held by it. It is also called alaya consciousness. Why? It is because this consciousness is absorbed by the physical body; it hides and stays in physical body as long as the body exists. Another name for this consciousness is mind. Why? All sights, sounds, smells, tastes, and contacts arise and accumulate because of this consciousness; they are nurtured by the consciousness and then grow.

"Broad Wisdom, relying on adana, the six roots, namely, the eye, ear, nose, tongue, body, and conscious roots, are established. They thus appear and begin to function. The combination of the conscious sphere, eye sphere, and the sight sphere will give rise to the eye consciousness while the perception or differentiation will operate along with it. The combination of the conscious sphere, ear sphere, and the sound sphere will give rise to the ear consciousness while the perception or differentiation will operate along with it. As the conscious, nose, tongue, or body sphere combines with correspondent smell, taste, and touch sphere will give rise to nose consciousness, tongue consciousness, or body consciousness respectively while the perception or differentiation will also operate along with each of them.

"Broad Wisdom, when the eye consciousness operates, there

will be only one differentiation operating simultaneously with it. When two, three, four, or five kinds of consciousness operate together, there will be only one differentiation operating with them also. Broad Wisdom, it is like a large waterfall. When the conditions are available for only one stream, there will be only one moving stream. When the conditions are available for two or more streams, there will be two or more moving streams, but the waterfall itself will continue falling down in a stable tempo uninterruptedly and endlessly regardless of the flowing waves. It is also like a clean and clear mirror. When the conditions are available for the arising of one image, there will be only one image. When the conditions are available for the arising of two or more images, there will be two or more images, but the mirror's face is still there as it is; it will not become an image itself, nor will it stop reflecting the objects. Therefore, Broad Wisdom, the adana consciousness is like the waterfall that provides a basis. When the conditions are ready for the arising of the eye consciousness, there will be only the eye consciousness that operates. When the conditions are sufficient for the arising of the ear consciousness, nose consciousness, tongue consciousness, body consciousness, and conscious consciousness, all these five kinds of consciousness will operate simultaneously.

"Broad Wisdom, as the bodhisattvas try to establish the secret skillfulness of the mind consciousness based on the knowledge of dharma dwelling, the Thus-Comers will not regard them as ones with all kinds of secret skillfulness of the mind consciousness. Broad Wisdom, as the bodhisattvas explore inside and do not see adana, alaya, the accumulation, the mind, the sight sphere and the eye consciousness, the sound sphere and the ear consciousness, the smell sphere and the nose consciousness, the taste sphere and the tongue consciousness, the contact sphere and the body consciousness, and the mental-image sphere and the conscious consciousness, the Thus-Comers will regard them as the bodhisattvas with the secret skillfulness of mind consciousness."

At that time, the World-Honored One reiterated the same meaning in verse:

Adana is very thin, subtle, and fathomless;
All seeds in it are like streams in a waterfall.
I do not teach this meaning to ignorant ordinary sentient
    beings
Because I fear they will differentiate and grasp it as selfness.

4

The Forms of All Dharmas

At that time, Virtue Base Great Bodhisattva asked the Buddha, "World-Honored One, you have mentioned about the bodhisattvas with skillfulness in various dharma forms. What are the bodhisattvas with skillfulness in dharma forms? Why do you establish the bodhisattvas as ones with skillfulness in dharma forms?"

The World-Honored One replied to Virtue Base Bodhisattva after hearing what he said, "Excellent! Excellent! Virtue Base, now you can ask Thus-Comer such a question of profound meaning. You ask this question because you are compassionate over all sentient beings of the worlds, including the heavenly beings, human beings, asuras, and so forth. You would like to bring benefits, peace, and happiness to all of them. Now listen to me carefully, I am going to teach you various dharma forms.

"There are three kinds of dharma forms: the form of universal attachment, the form of dependent origination, and the form of perfect realization.

"What is meant by the form of universal attachment? It means that the different natures of all dharmas are established with provisional names, followed by words and speeches. What is meant by the form of dependent origination? It means that the natures of all dharmas are caused by conditions. Because this dharma is existent, another dharma is existent; because this dharma arises, another dharma arises. It also means that ignorance causes action, action causes consciousness, and so forth, and all the dharmas thus caused will accumulate to form a great aggregation of suffering. What is meant by the form of perfect realization? It means the equality of the realness of all dharmas. If the bodhisattvas reflect correctly, bravely, diligently, and reasonably on realness, they will be able to thoroughly understand it. If they can further cultivate and learn it step by step, they will not only realize it, but also gradually attain the unsurpassed, perfect, and universal bodhi.

"Good gentleman, ones with eye disease will have cloudy vision, so is the form of universal attachment. Those with such vision will see the hair, circles around the hair, bees, flies, and lettuce differently, or will see the colors of the things in green, yellow, red, or white differently; so is the form of dependent origination. Ones with healthy eyes will see the world clearly and correctly; so is the form of perfect realization.

"Good gentleman, as the pure crystal blends with blue dye, it will look like a sky-blue jewel. People looking at it will be confused, and will mistake it for real jewel. As the pure crystal blends with red dye, it will look like amber, and people will mistake it for real amber. If the pure crystal blends with green dye, it will look like emerald, and people will mistake it for emerald. If it blends with yellow dye, it will look like gold, and people will mistake it for gold. Therefore, Virtue Base Bodhisattva, like all dyes' colors that are reflected in crystals, so are the habits of language and speech held by universal attachment in dependent origination. Like the images which the people mistake for blue jewel, amber, shell, and gold, so are the illusions held by universal attachment in dependent origination. Like the crystal that is pure as it is, so is the dependent origination. Like the phenomena appearing in the pure crystal at all times that are unreal, so is the attachment to dependent origination. As ones become aware that the varied colors manifested in the pure crystal are unreal and without self-natures at all times, they will achieve perfect realization.

"Furthermore, Virtue Base, as ones try to make forms correspondent with names, you must know that they fall in universal attachment. For them, dependent origination is also the object to which their universal attachment clings. As ones become free from attachment to dependent origination, they will attain perfect realization.

"Good gentleman, if the bodhisattvas can understand universal attachment as it really is based on the reality of dependent origination, they will understand that the dharmas are formless as they really are. If the bodhisattvas can understand dependent origination as it really is, they will also realize how the forms of the dharmas are contaminated. If the bodhisattvas can realize perfectly the dharmas as they really are, they will realize the pure forms of dharmas.

"Good gentleman, if the bodhisattvas can understand the formless dharmas as they really are through the reality of dependent origination, they will terminate the contaminated forms of dharmas and realize and attain the pure forms of dharmas. Therefore, Virtue Base, as the bodhisattvas realize universal attachment, dependent origination, and perfect realization as they really are, they will become aware of the formlessness, the contaminated forms, and the pure forms of dharmas as they really are. Because they have realized the formlessness of dharmas, they will terminate all contaminated forms of dharmas. Because they have terminated all contaminated forms of dharmas, they will realize all pure forms of dharmas. They are thus named the bodhisattvas with skillfulness in dharma forms."

At that time, the World-Honored One reiterated the same meaning in verse:

If we do not know the formlessness of dharmas
The contaminated forms of dharmas will not be terminated.
If we cannot terminate the contaminated forms of dharmas
The exquisite, subtle, and pure forms of dharmas will not be
*   realized.*
If we do not contemplate the faults of all actions
Our laziness and lack of self-restraint will do harm to sentient
*   beings.*
The slack and tired ones in meditation will become restless
They will attain nothing but miserably losing all!

The Phenomena of Selflessness

At that time, Ultimate Meaning Arising Great Bodhisattva said to the Buddha, "World-Honored One, I once stayed alone in a quiet place and thought that the World-Honored One has taught us through numberless gates about various aggregates, including their particular characteristics, forms of arising, forms of extinction, permanent cessation, and comprehensive knowledge.

"Like teaching about the aggregates, the World-Honored One has also taught about the particular characteristics, arising, extinction, permanent cessation, and comprehensive knowledge of the spheres, dependent origination, and various kinds of food.

"You have taught by means of numberless gates about the particular characteristics, comprehensive knowledge, permanent cessation, realization, cultivation, and learning of the noble truths. You have taught by means of numberless gates about all particular characteristics, natures, non-singular natures, permanent cessation, and comprehensive knowledge of various realms. You have also taught by means of numberless gates about the correct mindfulness, including its particular characteristics, the one who can deal with vexations and puzzles, the vexations and puzzles that one will deal with, and its cultivation and learning to make the positive things that have not happened happen and that have already happened increase and grow. You have also taught about the correct endeavors, bases of power, roots, powers, and the factors for enlightenment this way.

"You have taught through numberless gates about the noble eightfold path, including its particular characteristics, the one who will deal with vexations and puzzles, the vexations and puzzles that one will deal with, and its cultivation and learning to make the positive things that have not happened happen and that have already happened increase and grow. But on the other hand, World-Honored One, you have also said that all dharmas do not have self-natures; they are without arising and extinction; they are inherently tranquil; and their self-natures are in nirvana. I cannot understand the secret meanings implied by your saying. I am beseeching you to teach us the profound secret meanings implied by what you say that all dharmas do not have self-natures; they are without arising and extinction; they are inherently tranquil; and their self-natures are in nirvana."

At that time, the Buddha replied to Ultimate Meaning Arising Bodhisattva, "Excellent! Excellent! Your reflections are quite reasonable. It is very good that you can ask such a profound question. You are asking because you would like to bring benefits, justice, and happiness to innumerable sentient beings. It is because you are compassionate over all human beings, heavenly beings, asuras, and so forth that you want to bring them benefits, justice, peace, and happiness. Now please listen to me carefully, I am going to explain why all dharmas are without self-natures, arising, and extinction; why they are inherently tranquil and their self-natures are in nirvana. You must know, Ultimate Meaning Arising, I say that all dharmas are without self-natures based on the implied meanings of the three kinds of selflessness: phenomena are selfless, arising is selfless, and the ultimate meaning is also selfless.

"Good gentleman, why are the phenomena of all dharmas without self-natures? It is because the phenomena of all dharmas are caused by universal attachment. Why? The phenomena of the dharmas are provisionally established by provisional names rather than by their particular characteristics. That's why I say that the phenomena are without self-natures.

"Why is the arising of all dharmas without self-nature? It is because all dharmas are dependently originated. Why? All dharmas become existent out of the combination of causes and conditions; they do not exist inherently. That's why I say that the arising of all dharmas is without self-nature.

"Why is the ultimate meaning without self-nature? Because the arising of all dharmas is without self-nature, all dharmas are named without self-natures. The truth that all dharmas are dependently originated is also named the ultimate meaning without self-nature. Why? I make it clear that the pure perceived images belong to the ultimate meaning without self-nature. Even in the impure phenomena of dependent origination, the truth that the ultimate meaning is without self-nature is still there. Furthermore, the perfect realization of all dharmas is also named the ultimate meaning without self-nature. Why? 'All dharmas are without selfness' is named 'the ultimate meaning'; it is also named the nature without self-nature. This is the ultimate truth of the phenomena of all dharmas in which no self-nature is manifested. The name of the ultimate meaning without self-nature is established because of this cause and condition.

"Good gentleman, like the illusory flowers in the sky, so are the phenomena without self-natures. Like empty space, so are the phenomena of all matters without natures wherever they appear. You must know that the ultimate meaning without selfness is so named because the dharmas are without self-natures wherever they appear. Good gentleman, I am adopting the implied meanings of these three kinds of selflessness to demonstrate that all dharmas are without self-natures.

"Ultimate Meaning Arising, you must know that I have adopted the implied meaning of the phenomena without self-natures to say that all dharmas do not have arising and extinction; they are intrinsically tranquil and their natures are inherently in a state of nirvana. Why? If the particular characteristics of all dharmas are nonexistent, then they will not have arising or extinction. If they do not have arising and extinction, they are inherently tranquil and their self-natures are in nirvana. Why? The ultimate meaning of selflessness as demonstrated by the fact that all dharmas are without self-natures shows that the real essence of all dharmas resides firmly and permanently in nonaction at all times. It does not correspond with any impure and flawed things. Because it resides firmly and permanently in nonaction and has no arising, it does not disappear either. Because the real essence of all dharmas does not correspond with any impure or flawed things, they are intrinsically tranquil and their natures are inherently in a state of nirvana.

"Furthermore, Ultimate Meaning Arising, I establish the

three kinds of self-natures as selfless not because the sentient beings have contemplated the self-nature held by universal attachment as self-nature, or because they have contemplated the self-natures of dependent origination and the perfect realization as self-nature. It is rather because the sentient beings have added their universal attachment to the self-nature of dependent origination and perfect realization.

"Because the sentient beings are attached to the phenomena of self-natures, they initiate speeches to express the self-natures of dependent origination and perfect realization. Again and again, more permeations of speeches arise to influence their perceptions, and hidden vexations will also follow. This turns out more attachments to the self-natures of dependent origination and perfect realization. These causes and conditions will bring about more arisings in the future. It is also because of this reason that they will be contaminated by filthy vexations, filthy karmas, or filthy arising, and thus will drift endlessly in birth and death in the hells (naraka), the realm of animals, the realm of hungry ghosts; or will be reborn as heavenly beings, asuras, and human beings. They will suffer from various pains, sorrows, and worries incessantly.

"Furthermore, Ultimate Meaning Arising, some sentient beings have not planted virtuous roots and purified hindrances since the time unknown, they do not become mature, nor have they cultivated the definitive superior understanding and accumulated sufficient virtues and wisdom for spiritual nourishment. I will teach these sentient beings the selflessness of arising so they will understand that all arising phenomena are impermanent, changeable, and will decay. Then they will stay alert, become disgusted with all superficial phenomena, refrain from doing evil things, and diligently cultivate and learn the virtuous dharmas. Because of practicing the virtuous causes, they will be able to plant the virtuous seeds that they have not planted yet, purify the obstacles that they have not purified yet, and make incessant efforts to become more and more mature. Because of this cause and condition, they will spend more time to cultivate the definitive superior understanding and also accumulate more virtues and wisdom to nurture their spiritual growth.

"Although these sentient beings have planted virtuous roots and accumulated the two kinds of nutrients for cultivation: merits-virtues and wisdom, they have not fully understood the selflessness of phenomena and other two kinds of ultimate meaning of selflessness: the selflessness of dependent origination and the selflessness of perfect realization. They are not disgusted with all phenomena correctly; they do not get rid of desires correctly; they have not attained right liberation; they are not free from the contamination of vexations; they are not free from the contamination of karmas; and they are not free from the contamination of all kinds of arising. So the Thus-Comer will further teach these sentient beings the essential meanings of the dharmas, namely, the selflessness of all phenomena and the selflessness of the ultimate meaning, so they will become disgusted with all phenomena, stay far away from desires correctly, and attain right liberation. They will thus be able to transcend all contaminations of vexations, karmas, and arising.

"After hearing the dharma taught by the Thus-Comer, the sentient beings will develop correct belief in and understanding of the selflessness of phenomena and the selflessness of ultimate meaning in the selflessness of arising. They will also reflect on, analyze, intelligently judge, and thoroughly understand them. Through the realization of dependent origination, they will get rid of universal attachment to the images of self-natures. Because their speeches do not permeate and influence their knowledge and enlightenment any more, and because they have stayed away from the hidden seeds of vexations, they will not be attached to the phenomena of dependent origination. Owing to the power of knowledge and wisdom in dealing with the present dharmas, they are able to permanently cease the causes for the effects to come in the future. Because of this cause and condition, the sentient beings will become disgusted with all phenomena, get rid of desires, attain liberation, and completely stay away from the contamination of vexations, karmas, and arising.

"Furthermore, Ultimate Meaning Arising, the sentient beings with voice-hearer [sravaka] inclination will be able to follow this path to attain the ultimate peace and stability in nirvana. The sentient beings with self-enlightened one [pratyekabuddha] inclination and those with Thus-Comer [tathagata] inclination will also be able to do so. This is the only exquisite and pure path that all voice-hearers, self-enlightened ones, and bodhisattvas share and no other path is equivalent to this one. That is why I say that in the implied secret meaning, there is only one path and one vehicle. But this does not mean that all sentient beings, all species, all castes, the slow learners, the average learners, and the sharp learners are without differences.

"Good gentleman, although the Buddhas have made every effort to educate and guide those long-determined voice-hearer pursuers, I do not think that they will easily convert to the pursuit of anuttara-samyak-sambodhi. Why? It is because they have inferior intention and their compassion is slight; besides, they are afraid of various kinds of suffering. Because of their weak compassion, they are not used to do things beneficial for others. For fear of suffering, they do not vow to initiate actions beneficial for others. I will not say that the ones who have turned away from doing things beneficial for others will be dedicated to the attainment of anuttara-samyak-saṃbodhi. That is why they are classified as the practitioners with voice-hearer inclination. If they decide to convert and seek the ultimate great bodhi, I will also call them bodhisattva. Why? Once they become liberated from vexations and are awakened to the Buddhas' teachings, their minds will also be relieved from the barriers caused by their limited knowledge and view. But because the efforts they made previously were motivated by self-interest, namely, liberating themselves from the obstacles of vexations, the Thus-Comer still classifies them as the ones with voice-hearer inclination.

"Ultimate Meaning Arising, this is how various kinds of sentient beings differ in understanding and attaining vinaya [the precept] that I have set up and taught well, and of the virtuous dharmas that I have taught with my purest and most joyful intentions.

"Good gentleman, the Thus-Comer has also taught in the non-ultimate-meaning sutras the essential meanings of the dharma implicitly and say that all dharmas are without self-natures; all dharmas do not arise and extinguish; all dharmas are intrinsically tranquil; and the self-natures of all dharmas are in nirvana.

"If the sentient beings have planted the high-level virtuous seeds, cleared various barriers, grown continuously and become more mature, cultivated definitive superior understandings of these sutras, and accumulated merits, virtues, and wisdom as superior nourishment for growth; and if they can also listen to and accurately understand the profound secret meanings implied in my teachings, develop deep belief in and understanding of the dharma, and thoroughly grasp its meanings as they really are without upside-down views, then they will realize the ultimate wisdom quickly. They will also in my place develop deep and pure belief, and get to know that the Thus-Comer, One Worthy of Offerings, Perfectly and Universally Enlightened One is the holy one who has been fully awakened to all dharmas.

"Some sentient beings have planted the high-level virtuous roots, cleared all barriers, matured and grown continuously, and cultivated the definitive superior understanding well. Although they have not accumulated sufficient superior bliss, virtues, and wisdom for nursing the cultivation, they are the sort of straightforward personality. Although they cannot make wise judgment, they are not attached to incorrect views. Although they cannot fully understand the profound meanings implied in my words, they are whole-heartedly willing to learn and understand, and believe that these sutras are the words of the Buddhas correspondent with the very profound and subtle truth of emptiness. They are also aware that the truths contained in these sutras do not fall in the category of thinking, but go beyond thinking, so are difficult to investigate and understand by reflection. They know that the texts are subtle, elegant, detailed, and comprehensive, only the most intelligent ones can grasp them well. They are humble and willing to stay in the truths of the sutras. They say that the Buddhas' bodhi is the uppermost wisdom, and the dharma nature is extremely profound. They say that these teachings can be really and fully understood by the

Buddhas only, but not by the people like us. They also say that the Buddhas have given the correct dharma teachings for the sentient beings with definitive superior understanding. But in comparison with the Buddhas' limitless knowledge and views, the ordinary sentient beings are just like the footprints of an ox. Although they are able to respectfully lecture for others on these sutras; write, protect, read, spread, and sincerely make offerings to them; and accept, recite, and review them; they are still unable to initiate additional efforts with their way of cultivation. Therefore they cannot fully understand my words of the fathomless secret meanings. But because of the causes and conditions mentioned above, they are able to continuously accumulate merits and wisdom so as to nurture their cultivation and make the immature mature.

"Some sentient beings cannot accumulate the superior merits and wisdom; they are not straightforward in personality either. Although they can judge and make decision, they are attached to their own views. Therefore, when hearing my dharma teachings, they cannot accurately understand the hidden meanings implied in my words. Although they believe what I say and try to understand them, they are attached to the surface meanings of the words and assert that all dharmas definitely do not have self-nature, arising, and extinction; and that all dharmas are definitely tranquil and in nirvana. Because of this cause and condition, they develop a point of view that all dharmas are nonexistent and without phenomena and insist that all phenomena are formless. They thus argue against the form of universal attachment, the form of dependent origination, and the form of perfect realization. Why? They say that the universal attachment is set up based on dependent origination and perfect realization; as the dependent origination and perfect realization are formless, universal attachment should also be formless. It is based on this reasoning that they wrongly argue against the existence of the three forms. They have viewed correct dharma as correct dharma, but have also mistaken incorrect meanings for correct meanings. Because they have initiated the belief in the dharma and try to understand it, their blessings and virtues grow and increase. Because they have mistaken incorrect meanings for correct meanings and are attached to incorrect understanding, their knowledge and wisdom diminish. Because their knowledge and wisdom diminish, they will regress and lose numberless broad and great virtuous dharmas.

"Furthermore, some sentient beings have heard the statements made by ones who view correct dharma as correct dharma but mistake incorrect meanings for correct meanings. If these sentient beings follow such incorrect views, they will also view correct dharma as correct dharma but mistake incorrect meanings for correct meanings. Because of this cause and condition, they will regress in cultivation and their virtuous dharmas will diminish.

"Some sentient beings do not follow such views. They happen to hear the saying, 'All dharmas do not have self-natures, arising, and extinction; they are inherently tranquil and always in nirvana.' After hearing this, they are frightened and assert that these words are given by evil demons instead of the Buddha. Dominated by this thought they will slander the sutras, and thus will lose much and invite great karmic hindrances in cultivation. Because of this reason, I will say that those who view all forms as formless and mistake incorrect meanings for correct meanings will inevitably drive numberless sentient beings and themselves into great karmic hindrances.

"Good gentleman, some sentient beings have neither planted virtuous roots nor removed and purified obstacles. They neither continue to grow nor attain superior understanding. They have not accumulated merits and wisdom and their personality is not straightforward. They have the ability to make choice but are attached to their own views. These sentient beings will not accurately and fully understand the implied meanings in my words, nor believe in the dharma. They mistake correct dharma for incorrect dharma and correct meanings for incorrect meanings. They insist that the correct views are not correct, the truth is not true, and further assert that the correct dharma and the correct meanings are taught by evil demons instead of the Buddha. They thus slander the sutras and argue against them, and say that they are spurious, so try all possible ways to destroy them. They also oppose the ones who believe in and understand the sutras. They have had many karmic hindrances already; now because of what they are doing, their hindrances increase. Owing to the accumulation of hindrances, they will suffer for hundreds of thousands of koti nayuta kalpas and not be able to get rid of them.

"Good gentleman, I have taught and set up the precepts very well with my purest and most joyful intention for the sentient beings, and each hearer has gotten different understanding and interpretation to satisfy his or her need.

At that time, the World-Honored One reiterated the same meaning in verse:

All dharmas are without natures.
They do not arise or extinguish and are inherently tranquil.
The natures of all dharmas are always in nirvana.
How can the wise words be without implied secret meanings?

The ultimate meaning of arising phenomena is selflessness.
This meaning I have demonstrated in my teachings.
Ones who cannot know the Buddha's secret meaning
Will go astray from correct path and cannot move forward.

For the pure practitioners pursuing the pure path,
There is no other path than this one.
Therefore I have only set up one vehicle,
Although it does not mean all sentient beings do not differ.

Among innumerable sentient beings in all realms,
Some are only interested in relieving themselves.
Those who pursue nirvana with great compassion and
courage
And never turn away from sentient beings are unusual and
invaluable.

In exquisite and inconceivable realm of flawlessness,
Various kinds of liberation are equal.
Puzzles and suffering will cease once justice prevails
Permanence and Happiness are two terms for this meaning.

At that time, Ultimate Meaning Arising Bodhisattva said to the Buddha again, "World-Honored One, the implied meanings of the Buddha's words are incredible and unusual. The Buddha's words are subtle and subtlest, exquisite and most exquisite, and fathomless and most fathomless; they are difficult and most difficult to understand. My understanding of the World-Honored One's teaching is: when perceiving the universally attached images of the dharmas, we establish provisional names for each of them. We establish the names such as the aggregate of matters, the self-nature of matters, and the particular characteristics of matters. We also establish the arising and extinction of matters, the permanent extinction of vexations caused by matters, and the comprehensive understanding of the self-nature and different characteristics of matters. This is named the form of universal attachment. Because of this reason, the World-Honored One has established the phenomena of all dharmas as without self-natures. As we contemplate the universally-attached phenomena and can tell the images they rely on, we will realize the form of dependent origination. The World-Honored One thus has established the arising of all dharmas and the ultimate meaning as without self-natures. Now I can realize what the World-Honored One says that in the process of perceiving phenomena, the images thus derived in universal attachment are not real. To realize that the self-natures of the dharmas are selfless is to stay with the pure and selfless realness of all dharmas and this realization is named perfect realization. This is what the World-Honored One has established as the ultimate meaning without self-nature.

"Like the aggregate of matter, so the rest of aggregates can also be elaborated this way. Like various aggregates, so each of the twelve spheres, twelve chains of dependent arising, four kinds of food, six realms, and eighteen realms can also be elaborated this way. Now I can realize the meaning taught by the World-

Honored One; that is, if the perceived images of the noble truth of suffering, the comprehensive knowledge of suffering, the form of its self-nature, and the different forms of suffering are established and the provisional names are given to them, then there is the form of universal attachment. In order to remind us of the truth, the World-Honored One thus sets up the phenomena of all dharmas as without self-natures. If we can perceive the images and tell how they are universally attached, then we will realize the form of dependent origination. The World-Honored One thus has established the arising of all dharmas and the ultimate meaning as without self-natures in order to remind us of the truth. Now I can realize the meaning taught by the World-Honored One. If we can perceive the universally attached images as unreal, that is, if we can realize the pure realness of the selflessness of the phenomena and the selflessness of all dharmas, we will realize the form of perfect realization. The World-Honored One thus has set up the nature of the ultimate meaning as without self-nature.

"Like the noble truth of suffering, so we will also elaborate the rest of the noble truths. Like the noble truths, so the mindfulness, correct endeavors, bases of power, roots, powers, factors for enlightenment, and the noble path will also be elaborated. Now I can understand the meaning taught by the World-Honored One. When perceiving the universally attached images of the dharmas, the provisional names are given to the correct meditation, the subject who can improve and correct, the objects that will be improved and corrected, the positive actions that have not yet happened should be made happen, the positive things that have already happened should be expanded and proliferated, as well as their particular characteristics and differences. This is named the form of universal attachment. The World-Honored One thus has established all dharmas as without self-natures. As we contemplate the images held by universal attachment, we will be able to realize the principle of dependent origination. The World-Honored One thus has established the arising of all dharmas and the ultimate meaning as without self-natures. Now I can understand the meaning taught by the World-Honored One. If we can perceive the universally-attached images as unreal, that is, if we can realize the pure realness of the selfless self-nature and the selfless dharmas, then we realize the form of perfect realization. The World-Honored One thus has established the self-nature of the ultimate meaning of all dharmas as selfless.

"World-Honored One, like the medicine named Pishibu that is compatible with all other medicines and can be used for specific diseases or as panacea, so the Buddha's teachings of the ultimate meanings that all dharmas are without self-natures, without arising and extinction, and inherently tranquil and their self-natures are always in nirvana, are compatible with the sutras of non-ultimate meanings.

"World-Honored One, a primer with one unified essence can be used for painting in green, yellow, red, or white; it is not only compatible with the painting but also can make it more brilliant and resplendent. So are the Buddha's ultimate meanings that all dharmas are without self-natures, without arising and extinction, and inherently tranquil and their self-natures are always in nirvana. The meanings of one essence spread in the sutras of non-ultimate meanings. They are not only compatible with the sutras of non-ultimate meanings, but also make them more significant. World-Honored One, the ghee has only one essence and can be used to mix with other tasty food. Meals, cookies, and fruits, for instance, remain distinct but also become more delicious when they are mixed with the ghee. So is the World-Honored One's teaching of the ultimate meanings when he says that all dharmas are without self-natures, without arising and extinction, and inherently tranquil and their self-natures are always in nirvana. The ultimate meanings are compatible with the non-ultimate meanings. When placed in the sutras of the non-ultimate meanings, the ultimate meanings will bring about superior joy for the cultivators. World-Honored One, empty space spreads all over the world and shares the same taste with all beings in the world, but it will not hinder the operations or the activities of the world. So are the World-Honored Ones' teachings of the ultimate meanings when he says that all dharmas are without self-natures, without arising and extinction, and inherently tranquil and their self-natures are always in nirvana. The teachings of the ultimate meanings spreading all over the sutras of the non-ultimate meanings will not hinder the cultivation undertaken by the voice-hearers, self-enlightened ones, and great-vehicle practitioners."

After hearing these words, the World-Honored One praised Ultimate Meaning Arising Bodhisattva, "Excellent! Excellent! What a good gentleman. Now you understand the profound and secret meanings implied by the Buddha's words. It is wonderful that you can further interpret the meanings with the similes, such as the medicine, the prime color for painting, the ghee for food, and the vast empty space. Ultimate Meaning Arising, what you say is correct. All of you should accept and practice this teaching of the ultimate meanings."

At that time, Ultimate Meaning Arising Bodhisattva said

to the Buddha again, "World-Honored One, when you attained the unsurpassed enlightenment, you began to turn the dharma wheel. You taught the four noble truths to the voice-hearer pursuers in Deer Park where five hundred flying celestial beings once fell. Your teachings were very exquisite, unique, and rare; no other human beings or heavenly beings could do this. But the dharma wheel you turned at that time was not that of the ultimate meanings and thus invited arguments and provided room for the more ultimate teachings to come in later times.

"World-Honored One, during the second period of your teaching, you turned the dharma wheel and taught the great-vehicle practitioners in a secret way, saying that all dharmas are without self-natures, arising, and extinction; they are inherently tranquil and their self-natures are in nirvana. Your teachings at that time were also very exquisite, unique, and rare, but still were not the ultimate meanings, and thus still invited arguments and provided room for the more ultimate teachings to come in later times.

"World-Honored One, now it is the third period of your teaching; you are turning the dharma wheel for the aspirants of different vehicles. You are now teaching explicitly to say that all dharmas are without self-natures, arising, and extinction; they are inherently tranquil and their self-natures are in nirvana. Your current teachings are the most exquisite and most unusual ones; they are really the ultimate meanings; they are unsurpassed and do not invite any controversial argument.

"World-Honored One, if the good gentlemen and gentlewomen can listen to, believe in, understand, write, protect, embrace, make offerings to, propagate, recite, cultivate, learn, reflect reasonably on, and practice with additional effort the fathomless ultimate meanings of your teaching—all dharmas are without self-natures, arising, and extinction; they are inherently tranquil; and their self-natures are in nirvana—then how will they be blessed?"

The Buddha replied to Ultimate Meaning Arising Bodhisattva, "Ultimate Meaning Arising, the blessings gained by these good gentlemen and gentlewomen will be numberless and countless, even more than one can imagine. Let me explain briefly for you. It is like the dust in the paw in contrast with the soil of the entire earth. The former is smaller than the latter one by one hundredth, one thousandth, one hundred thousandth, and one upanisadam-api. It is also like the water contained in an ox's footprint in comparison with the water contained in the four seas. The former is smaller than the latter by one hundredth, one thousandth, one hundred thousandth, and one upanisandam-api. In comparison, the merits and virtues gained by hearing, believing, understanding, and practicing the non-ultimate meanings will be much less than those obtained by hearing, believing, understanding, and practicing the ultimate meanings by one hundredth, one thousandth, one hundred thousandth, and one upanisandam-api."

Ultimate Meaning Arising Bodhisattva then asked the Buddha again, "World-Honored One, what name is this dharma gate of explaining the profound secret? How should we follow and practice this dharma gate?"

The Buddha replied to Ultimate Meaning Arising Bodhisattva, "Good gentleman, this dharma gate is named the teaching of the superior ultimate meaning. All of you should follow and practice this ultimate meaning."

When the Buddha was teaching the superior ultimate meaning, six hundred thousand sentient beings were inspired and determined to aspire to anuttara-samyak-saṃbodh; three hundred thousand voice-hearers stayed far away from defilements and attained the pure dharma eye; one hundred fifty thousand voice-hearers were permanently liberated from all flaws; and seventy-five thousand bodhisattvas attained the dharma forbearance of nonarising.

The Ultimate Meaning of Yoga

At that time, Maitreya Great Bodhisattva asked the Buddha, "World-Honored One, how should the bodhisattvas rely and dwell when cultivating samatha and vipasyana of great vehicle?"

The Buddha replied to Maitreya Bodhisattva, "Good gentleman, you must know that the bodhisattvas should rely on and dwell in the provisionally established dharma and vow never to regress from pursuing anuttara-samyak-sambodhi when cultivating samatha and vipasyana of great vehicle."

Maitreya Bodhisattva asked the Buddha again, "The World-Honored One has taught the four kinds of knowing process: The knowing process with the images of differentiation caused by conceptual thinking and reasoning, the knowing process without the images of differentiation caused by conceptual thinking and reasoning, the knowing process covering various phenomena and characteristics of many dharmas simultaneously, and the knowing process of the cultivation leading to perfect accomplishment. In regard to these four processes, which are in the category of samatha? Which are in the category of vipasyana? Which are in both categories?"

The Buddha replied to Maitreya Bodhisattva, "Good gentleman, the knowing process without the images of differentiation caused by conceptual thinking and reasoning falls in the category of samatha. The knowing process with the images of differentiation caused by conceptual thinking and reasoning falls in the category of vipasyana. The knowing process covering various phenomena and characteristics of all dharmas and the knowing process of the cultivation leading to perfect accomplishment are in both categories."

Maitreya Bodhisattva asked the Buddha again, "World-Honored One, how can the bodhisattvas achieve samatha and master vipasyana by means of these four kinds of knowing process?"

The Buddha replied to Maitreya Bodhisattva, "Good gentleman, the dharma I teach provisionally established for the bodhisattvas includes twelve areas: texts (sutra), short verses (geya), prophecy (vyakarana), long verses (gatha), self-statement (udana), origins (nidana), similes (avadana), anecdotes (itivrttaka), past lives (jataka), broad teaching (vaipulya), unusual ways (abdhuta-dharma), and discourses (upadesa). The bodhisattvas should listen to and accept them well. They should get to know the words well, and reflect on the meanings thoroughly so as to develop positive views. They would better find a quiet place where they can stay alone to reflect on these teachings attentively and uninterruptedly so they will attain freedom and ease in body and mind through dwelling peaceful in correct actions. This is named samatha. This is the way the bodhisattvas should follow in pursuing samatha.

"After acquiring freedom and ease in body and mind, they will be able to move forward to examine and inquire into the images shown by positive reflection in samadhi. They will attain superior definitive understanding, and then get away from these images. In the known meanings of the images in samadhi, the practitioners should scrutinize and figure out all their characteristics from various perspectives, reflect on them comprehensively, and make correct, intelligent, and wise judgments as best as possible. They will undertake comprehensive in-depth investigations with patience, fondness, wise choice, correct views, and contemplation in the process. This is named vipasyana. It is through this approach that the bodhisattvas may master vipasyana."

Maitreya Bodhisattva asked the Buddha again, "World-Honored One, if the bodhisattvas have aimed at their minds as a target for examination and so forth, but have not obtained freedom and self-ease in their intentions, what will this mind be named?"

The Buddha replied, "Good gentleman, this will not be named the attentiveness to samatha; it will be named the intention compliant with the definitive understanding in samatha."

"World-Honored One, if the bodhisattvas have intended to examine images shown in samadhi but have not obtained freedom and self-ease in body and mind, what will this be named?"

"Good gentleman, this will not be named the attentiveness to vipasyana; it will be named the intention compliant with the definitive understanding of vipasyana."

Maitreya Bodhisattva asked the Buddha again, "World-Honored One, is the path of samatha different from the path of vipasyana? Are they not different?"

The Buddha replied, "Good gentleman, they are neither different nor not different. Why are they not different? It is because both vipasyana and samatha aim at the images of the mind. Why are they different? It is because vipasyana perceives and differentiates the images while samatha does not."

Maitreya Bodhisattva asked the Buddha again, "World-Honored One, are the images produced in the samadhi of vipasyana the same as the mind?"

The Buddha replied to Maitreya Bodhisattva, "Good gentleman, we should say that they are not different. Why? It is because all images come from the mind. Good gentleman, I will say that the known objects only reflect what the consciousness of the knowing subject perceives."

"World-Honored One, if these images are not different from the mind, how can this mind see this mind?"

"Good gentleman, the fact is that no dharma can really see another dharma. But as the mind starts something, images appear. Good gentleman, it is like a clear mirror that precisely and exactly reflects the matter in front of it, and the mirror remains as it is. As I see the images and say that they are apart from the mirror, it will be like saying that the images of the known objects are apart from this mind. That is why when something arises in the mind, it looks like some different images are appearing apart from the mind."

"World-Honored One, if the sentient beings incline to stay in the images created by the contact of the mind with matter and so forth, are these images not different from the mind?"

"Good gentleman, they are not different, but the ordinary people cannot understand the images as they really are; that is, they do not know that the images are merely the reflection of one's consciousness, therefore they have upside-down understanding."

Maitreya Bodhisattva asked the Buddha again, "World-Honored One, what is meant by saying that the bodhisattvas have cultivated vipasyana continuously?"

The Buddha replied to Maitreya Bodhisattva, "Good gentleman, it means that they have continuously intended to reflect on the images of mind only."

"World-Honored One, what is meant by saying that the bodhisattvas have cultivated samatha continuously?"

"Good gentleman, it means that they have continuously intended to reflect on the uninterrupted mind only."

"World-Honored One, what is meant by saying that the bodhisattvas have practiced samatha and vipasyana simultaneously?"

"Good gentleman, it means that they have maintained in correct concentration to reflect on one object."

"World-Honored One, what are the images of the mind?"

"Good gentleman, they are the perceived images caused by vipasyana in samadhi."

"World-Honored One, what is the uninterrupted mind?"

"Good gentleman, it means to keep paying attention to the images in samatha."

"World-Honored One, what is the mind with one single object?"

"Good gentleman, it means realizing the images in samadhi are merely the reflection of the mind; it also means after thorough understanding, they further undertake the reflection this way."

Maitreya Bodhisattva asked the Buddha again, "World-Honored One, how many kinds of vipasyana are there?"

The Buddha replied to Maitreya Bodhisattva, "Good gentleman, briefly speaking there are three kinds: the vipasyana with images, the vipasyana for general contemplation, and the vipasyana for specific investigation."

"What is the vipasyana with images?"

"It is the vipasyana that purely reflects on the images perceived in samadhi."

"What is the vipasyana for general contemplation?"

"It is the vipasyana with an intention to comprehensively reflect with wisdom on the unknown dharmas in order to fully understand them."

"What is the vapasyana for specific investigation?"

"It is the vipasyana with an intention to further investigate with wisdom the well-known dharmas in order to realize the ultimate liberation."

Maitreya Bodhisattva asked the Buddha again, "World-Honored One, how many kinds of samatha are there?"

The Buddha replied to Maitreya Bodhisattva, "Good gentleman, there are three kinds of samatha in accord with one's uninterrupted concentrative mind in undertaking vipasyana mentioned above. Samatha can also be classified into eight kinds: There is one kind of samatha for each stage from the first stage of meditation through the eighth stage of nonthinking and not nonthinking. In addition, there are four kinds of samatha: the samatha for immeasurable loving-kindness, the samatha for immeasurable compassion, the samatha for immeasurable joy, and the samatha for immeasurable equanimity."

Maitreya Bodhisattva asked the Buddha again, "World-

Honored One, it is said that there are the samatha and vipasyana in accord with dharmas and the samatha and vipasyana not in accord with dharmas. What do they mean?"

The Buddha replied to Maitreya Bodhisattva, "Good gentleman, the samatha and vipasyana in accord with dharmas means the bodhisattvas have followed the images of the dharmas they received or thought of to contemplate their meanings. The samatha and vipasyana not in accord with dharmas means the bodhisattvas have not followed the phenomena of dharmas they received or thought of, but followed the meanings given by others to contemplate. For instance, they will investigate 'bruises and pus'; 'all dharmas are in change'; 'all actions are painful'; 'all dharmas are selfless'; or 'ultimate tranquility in nirvana.' I will say that those practicing samatha and vipasyana in accord with dharmas are the sharp learners, while those practicing samatha and vipasyana not in accord with dharmas are the slow ones."

Maitreya Bodhisattva asked the Buddha again, "World-Honored One, there are the samatha and vipasyana based on individual approach and the samatha and vipasyana based on general approach. What do they mean?"

The Buddha replied to Maitreya Bodhisattva, "Good gentleman, 'the samatha and vipasyana based on individual approach' means the bodhisattvas cultivate samatha and vipasyana by thinking of what they have learned from each individual sutra, sastra, and so forth. 'The samatha and vipasyana based on general approach' means the bodhisattvas study many sutras, sastras, and so forth; they will put them together, reorganize and make them one, and reflect on them. They will further undertake reflection by following realness, approaching realness, and entering realness; they will also undertake reflection by following the bodhi, following nirvana, and approaching them. After entering all these virtuous dharmas, they will lecture on and teach numberless and countless virtuous dharmas for others. This is how the bodhisattvas reflect on and cultivate samatha and vipasyana based on general approach.

Maitreya Bodhisattva asked the Buddha again, "World-Honored One, there are the samatha and vipasyana based on minor general way, the samatha and vipasyana based on major general way, and the samatha and vipasyana based on number-less general ways. What do they mean?"

The Buddha replied to Maitreya Bodhisattva, "Good gentleman, 'the samatha and vipasyana based on minor general way' means the practitioners study one of the twelve areas of Buddha's teachings and contemplate all teachings in this area as one system. 'The samatha and vipasyana based on major general way' means the practitioners integrate all twelve areas of Buddha's teachings and contemplate them together as one single system. 'The samatha and vipasyana based on numberless general ways' means the practitioners integrate numberless dharma teachings given by the Buddha, numberless words and sentences of the dharma, and numberless inspirations and illuminations gained after learning and contemplate all of them together as one single system."

Maitreya Bodhisattva asked the Buddha again, "World-Honored One, how do we know that the bodhisattvas have acquired the samatha and vipasyana based on general approach?"

The Buddha replied, "There are five criteria for telling if they have attained it. The first is that when undertaking reflection, the bodhisattvas may feel the seeds of heavy vexations melt instantaneously upon every single reflection. The second is the bodhisattvas are able to get rid of all thoughts and enjoy the dharma delight. The third is the bodhisattvas are able to experience boundless rays of dharma light without differentiation in the ten directions. The fourth is the bodhisattvas will fulfill purity in what they are doing and feel that the form of nondifferentiation is present at all times. The fifth is the bodhisattvas will absorb previous positive effects and turn them into virtuous causes so as to fulfill the dharma body to come in the future."

Maitreya Bodhisattva asked the Buddha again, "World-Honored One, when do the bodhisattvas have smooth access to the samatha and vipasyana based on general approach? And when will they attain it?"

The Buddha replied, "Good gentleman, when reaching the first stage of ecstasy, the bodhisattvas will have good access to the samatha and vipasyana based on general approach. As entering the third stage of emitting light, they will attain the samatha and vipasyana based on general approach. Good gentleman, the novice bodhisattvas also should learn this way. They have not yet reached these stages, but I will encourage them to learn tirelessly; they should not give up or just fool around."

Maitreya Bodhisattva asked the Buddha again, "World-Honored One, in practicing samatha and vipasyana, what is the samadhi with general contemplation and specific investigation? What is the samadhi with specific investigation only? What is the samadhi without general contemplation and specific investigation?"

The Buddha replied to Maitreya Bodhisattva, "When searching and examining the images of dharmas in samatha and vipasyana and acquiring rough indications of perception, the bodhisattvas are undertaking the samadhi with general contemplation and specific investigation. If they have not had rough indications of perception but do have subtle and bright mindfulness, they are in the samadhi with investigation only. If they do not intend to perceive and contemplate the phenomena of dharmas in samatha and vipasyana, they are undertaking the samadhi without contemplation and investigation. Furthermore, good gentleman, if the bodhisattvas intend to look for something in samatha and vipasyana, they are undertaking the samadhi with contemplation and investigation. If they only investigate in samatha and vipasyana, they are undertaking the samadhi with investigation only. If they follow the general approach in samatha and vipasyana, they are undertaking the samadhi without contemplation and investigation."

Maitreya Bodhisattva asked the Buddha again, "World-Honored One, what is the way of calming down? What is the way of raising spirit? What is the way of renunciation?"

The Buddha replied to Maitreya Bodhisattva, "Good gentleman, when the bodhisattvas' minds fly too high and cannot concentrate, or they are afraid of being so, they may think about something sad or disgusting in order to calm themselves down. This is the way of calming down. When the bodhisattvas' minds sink and their spirits become low, or they are afraid of being so, they may think about something pleasant, or just temporarily turn away from what they are attentive to. This is the way of raising spirit. When ones are in concentration, investigation, or both, but are bothered and annoyed by vexations caused by very high or very low mood, they may just relax without pushing themselves tensely in any specific direction. This is the way of renunciation."

Maitreya Bodhisattva then asked the Buddha, "World-Honored One, some bodhisattvas practice samatha and vipasyana and can fully understand the dharmas and their meanings. How do they get to know the dharmas and the meanings of the dharmas?"

The Buddha replied to Maitreya Bodhisattva, "Good gentleman, the bodhisattvas get to know the dharmas through knowing five things. The first is to know the names. The second is to know the sentences. The third is to know the texts. The fourth is to know the particular features of the dharmas. The fifth is to know the common traits of the dharmas. What are the names? They are created provisionally to designate the pure or impure dharmas based on their supposed natures. What are the sentences? They are the assemblies of the words used to express the bases for establishing the pure and impure dharmas. What are the texts? They are the compositions of words including names and sentences. How can we understand individual things? We can understand individual things by studying their particular characteristics. How can we understand the common traits of dharmas? We can do it by studying and comparing all dharmas together. This is how the bodhisattvas get to know the dharmas.

"Good gentleman, the bodhisattvas get to fully understand the meanings of the dharmas in ten ways. The first is to know all particular natures of all kinds of dharmas. The second is to know the real natures of all dharmas. The third is to know the meanings of the perceiving subjects. The fourth is to know the meanings of the perceived objects. The fifth is to know the meanings of establishments. The sixth is to know the meanings of reception and usage. The seventh is to know the upside-down meanings. The eighth is to know the not upside-down meanings. The ninth is to know the meanings of mixture and contamination. The tenth is to know the meanings of purity.

"Good gentleman, to know all particular natures of all kinds of dharmas means to know all particular natures of all species or categories of pure and contaminated dharmas, such as the five aggregates, six inner spheres, six outer spheres, and so forth. The real natures of all dharmas indicate the realness of all pure and impure dharmas. This again comprises seven kinds. The first is the realness of drifting; this means that all existents do not really happen earlier or later. The second is the realness of phenomena; this means that the individual sentient beings and the rest of dharmas are without selfness. The third is the realness of perceiving process; this means that all phenomena are merely the manifestation of consciousness. The fourth is the realness of establishments; this indicates the noble truth of suffering that I teach. The fifth is the realness of negative actions; this means the noble truth of the cause of suffering that I teach. The sixth is the realness of purity; this means the noble truth of the cessation of suffering that I teach. The seventh is the realness of correct actions; this means the noble truth of the paths for the cessation of suffering that I teach.

"Based on the realness of drifting, the realness of establishments, and the realness of negative actions, all sentient beings are equal. Based on the realness of phenomena and the realness of perceiving process, all dharmas are equal. Based on the realness of purity, the voice-hearer bodhi, the self-enlightenment bodhi, and anuttara-samyak-saṃbodhi are equal. Based on the realness of correct actions, all kinds of wisdom absorbed by hearing correct dharma and practicing superior samatha and vipasyana are also equal.

"The meaning of perceiving subjects indicates the five physical spheres, namely the eye, ear, nose, tongue, and body spheres and the mind consciousness along with various mind dharmas. The meaning of perceived objects indicates the six outer spheres: the sight, sound, smell, taste, touch, and mental-image spheres. The perceiving subjects can also become the perceived objects. The meaning of establishments means the physical world, in which the realms of sentient beings are established; namely, one village and one field, one hundred villages and one hundred fields, one thousand villages and one thousand fields, and hundreds of thousands of villages and fields; one vast land that expands to the ocean side, one hundred vast lands, one thousand vast lands, and hundreds of thousands of vast lands that all expand to the ocean side; one continent of Jambudvipa, one hundred continents of Jambudvipa, one thousand continents of Jambudvipa, and hundreds of thousands of continents of Jambudvipa; one four-continent, one hundred four-continents, one thousand four-continents, and hundreds of thousands of four-continents; one small thousand-world, one hundred small thousand-worlds, one thousand small thousand-worlds, and hundreds of thousands of small thousand-worlds; one medium thousand-world, one hundred medium thousand-worlds, one thousand medium thousand-worlds, and hundreds of thousands of medium thousand-worlds; one large thousand-world, one hundred large thousand-worlds, one thousand large thousand-worlds, and hundreds of thousands of large thousand-worlds; one koti of world, one hundred kotis of world, one thousand kotis of world, and hundreds of thousands of kotis of worlds; and as many physical worlds in the ten directions as countless hundreds of thousands of minimum particles.

"The meaning of reception and usage means that the sentient beings receive and use various living supplies. The upside-down meaning means that the perceiving subjects have upside-down thoughts, minds, and views. For instance, they will mistake impermanence for permanence, suffering for pleasure, impurity for purity, and selflessness for selfness. These are the sentient beings with upside-down thoughts, minds, and views.

"The not upside-down meaning is contrary to the upside-down meaning. The not upside-down meaning can deal with and remove the upside-down meaning, so one should get to know it. The meaning of impurity indicates three kinds of contaminations in the three realms of the world; they are the contaminations of vexations, karmas, and arising in the realm of desire, the realm of form, and the realm of formlessness. The meaning of purity indicates the factors for enlightenment that one may adopt to get rid of the three kinds of contamination. Good gentleman, these ten kinds have covered all meanings.

"Furthermore, the bodhisattvas who can fully know the five kinds of meanings are also named knowing the meanings. What are the five kinds of meanings? The first is to know the things comprehensively. The second is to know the meanings comprehensively. The third is to know the causes comprehensively. The fourth is to know the effects comprehensively. And the fifth is to be awakened to and realize all of these meanings.

"Good gentleman, to know things comprehensively means the bodhisattvas know various aggregates, inner spheres, outer spheres, and so forth.

"To know meanings comprehensively means the bodhisattvas know various different kinds of meanings that they should know. These include the conventional meaning, ultimate meaning, merits and virtues, faults, conditions, and the world; the forms of arising, duration, and decay; illness and so forth; suffering, the cause of suffering, and so forth; realness, reality, dharma realm, and so forth. They also include the elaborated, lengthy, or succinct expression; saying yes definitely to correct questions; saying yes to correct questions but saying no to incorrect questions, and explaining why; replying by asking; giving no hint or answer; teaching in a subtle and hidden way, or in an explicit way, and so forth.

"To know causes comprehensively means to realize and absorb the first two factors for enlightenment, namely, the four bases of mindfulness and the four correct endeavors.

"To know effects comprehensively means to know the permanent termination of greed, anger, and ignorance as the effects gained by the sramanas. This also means to know the effects of cultivation either shared by Thus-Comers and voice-hearers or just possessed by Thus-Comers only; the effects belonging to the world and beyond the world; and the merits and virtues that the practitioners will realize.

"To become awakened to all things mentioned above means that after realizing and attaining the perfect knowledge of liberation, the bodhisattvas should lecture on and propagate the dharma extensively, elaborate and explain it for others. Good gentleman, these five kinds of meaning comprise all correct meanings of the truth.

"Furthermore, good gentleman, if the bodhisattvas know four kinds of meaning, they are named knowing the meanings of the truth. What are the four kinds of meaning? The first is that our minds always reach out, perceive, and become attached to all dharmas. The second is that our minds always receive stimuli from dharmas and thus experience various feelings. The third is that our minds cannot only perceive, but also think about the dharmas through a process of reasoning, analysis, and so forth. The fourth is the meanings of purity and impurity. Good gentleman, these four kinds of meaning also comprise all meanings.

"Furthermore, good gentleman, if the bodhisattvas know three kinds of meaning, they are named knowing the meanings. What are these three kinds of meaning? The first is the meaning of the words. The second is the meaning of the meanings. The third is the meaning of the realms.

"Good gentleman, the meaning of the words indicates the meaning of the names, the combination of the names, and so forth.

"The meaning of the meanings has ten kinds: the first is reality; the second is comprehensive knowledge; the third is permanent termination; the fourth is realization; the fifth is cultivation and learning; the sixth is the differences of the five kinds of meaning mentioned above; the seventh is the interaction between the dharmas to be relied on and the dharmas that rely; the eighth is the hinderance to comprehensive knowledge, and so forth; the ninth is the dharma compliant with comprehensive knowledge, and so forth; the tenth is the merits and virtues caused by the comprehensive knowledge and the faults caused by the not comprehensive knowledge.

"The meaning of the realms indicates the five realms: the physical world, the sentient beings, the dharmas, ones who need guidance and instruction, and ones who can adopt expedient and effective ways to guide and teach others. Good gentleman, these five meanings also comprise all kinds of meaning."

Maitreya Bodhisattva asked the Buddha again, "World-Honored One, there are the wisdom formed through hearing, the wisdom formed through thinking, and the wisdom formed through cultivation of samatha and vipasyana. What are their differences?"

The Buddha replied, "Good gentleman, ones who form wisdom through hearing rely on words. They have tried to understand what they heard, but they are unable to go beyond the surface meanings of the words. For them the reality has not shown yet. They are already in compliance with liberation, but have not realized its meaning as it really is. Ones who form wisdom through thinking also rely on words, but they can grasp underlying meanings. The reality has not shown yet for them. They can stay in liberation, but still cannot realize its meaning as it really is. Ones who attain wisdom through cultivation of samatha and vipasyana rely on words, but they are not confined by words. They either follow or go beyond others' sayings. They understand underlying meanings. As the images appear in samadhi harmoniously interacting with the objects investigated, the reality will appear as it really is. They are able to stay in liberation and realize the meaning of liberation. These are the differences among these three kinds of knowing the meanings."

Maitreya Bodhisattva asked the Buddha again, "World-Honored One, the bodhisattvas who cultivate samatha and vipasyana will know the dharmas and the meanings. But what is intelligence? What is view?"

The Buddha replied to Maitreya Bodhisattva, "Good gentleman, I have used innumerable approaches to teach people the difference between intelligence and view. Let me tell you briefly about it today. Intelligence indicates all sorts of exquisite wisdom attained through the cultivation of samatha and vipasyana based on general approach, while view indicates all sorts of exquisite wisdom attained through the cultivation of samatha and vipasyana based on individual approach."

Maitreya Bodhisattva asked the Buddha again, "World-Honored One, when cultivating samatha and vipasyana, how do the bodhisattvas concentrate? What images will they cast off? And how?"

The Buddha replied to Maitreya Bodhisattva, "Good gentleman, if the bodhisattvas concentrate on realness, they will be able to cast off the images of dharmas and the images of meanings. As ones do not intend to attain the names and the individual natures of the names, and do not contemplate the images on which the names rely, they will be able to cast off the images. It is the same for the sentences and texts. They can also cast off the images of the realms if they are not attached to the attainment of the realms and their natures, or if they do not contemplate the images on which the realms rely."

"World-Honored One, when realizing the meaning and form of realness, can the images of realness be cast off?"

"Good gentleman, in the meaning of the realness that one realizes, there is neither image nor attainment, so what will be cast off? Good gentleman, once the bodhisattvas realize the meaning of realness, they will be able to subjugate all the images of dharmas and the images of meanings; no any other dharma can subjugate this realization."

"World-Honored One, you have given similes saying that it is not adequate to look at your face in the turbid water, the unclean mirror, or the pond with spring flowing out. Those who say they can see their faces in turbid water and so forth will be in conflict with what you say. Therefore, people will not be able to see the realness of the dharmas until they have cultivated and purified their minds. Based on this saying, how can people contemplate and investigate their minds? On what realness is this saying based?"

"Good gentleman, people can contemplate their minds by hearing the truth, reflecting on the truth, and cultivating the truth. I say this based on the realness of the perception process."

"World-Honored One, when working diligently with additional effort to cast off various images, what images are particularly difficult to cast off by the bodhisattvas who have already known the dharmas and the meanings? What can cast off these images?"

"Good gentleman, there are ten kinds of images difficult to cast off. They can be cast off by emptiness. The first are the images of words caused by realizing the dharmas and meanings. These can be removed by emptiness of all dharmas.

"The second are the images of recurrent cycle of arising, duration, decay, and extinction caused by realizing the realness of establishments. These images can be removed by emptiness of form and emptiness of nontemporality.

"The third are the images of body attachment and self-conceit caused by realizing the perceiving subjects. Such images can be removed by internal emptiness and emptiness of nonattainment.

"The fourth are the images of grasping property caused by realizing the perceived objects. Such images can be removed by external emptiness.

"The fifth are the images of inner peace and comfort and

the images of outer exquisiteness and purity caused by realizing the reception of living supplies and services offered by men and women. Such images can be removed by internal-external emptiness and emptiness of original nature.

"The sixth are the numberless images caused by realizing the establishments. Such images can be removed by emptiness of space.

"The seventh are the images of inner tranquility and liberation caused by realizing formlessness. Such images can be removed by emptiness of conditioned phenomena.

"The eighth are the images of formlessness of individual sentient beings, selflessness of the dharmas, consciousness only, and ultimate meaning caused by realizing realness. Such images can be removed by emptiness in the final analysis, emptiness of selflessness, emptiness of selfless self-nature, and emptiness of ultimate reality.

"The ninth are the images of unconditioned reality and changelessness caused by realizing pure realness. Such images can be removed by emptiness of unconditioned reality and emptiness of changelessness.

"The tenth are the images of empty natures caused by intentional reflection on emptiness. Such images can be removed by emptiness of emptiness."

"World-Honored One, when removing these ten kinds of images, what will be really removed? From what images will bodhisattvas be liberated?"

"Good gentleman, the mental images in samadhi will be removed. Once the bodhisattvas are relieved from the images of defiled bondages, these images will also be removed. Good gentleman, you must know that as one kind of emptiness is more powerful for removing certain kind of images, it does not imply that this kind of emptiness is not applicable for removing other kinds of images. For example, ignorance also causes the arising of the defiled dharmas such as birth, old age, and death, but it is more powerful for causing action than others because it is closely affiliated with it. This principle can be generalized to other cases."

At that time, Maitreya Bodhisattva asked the Buddha again, "World-Honored One, what is the general nature of emptiness that will allow the bodhisattvas not to lose or destroy the nature and form of emptiness when they realize emptiness and get rid of arrogance?"

After hearing this question, the Buddha praised Maitreya Bodhisattva, "Excellent! Excellent! Good gentleman, now you finally ask such a queston with profound meaning so that the bodhisattvas will not lose or destroy the nature and form of emptiness. Why? Good gentleman, those who lose or destroy the nature and form of emptiness will also lose or destroy great vehicle. So, you must listen carefully to what I am going to say. Good gentleman, to stay far away from universal attachment to various pure and impure images in dependent origination and perfect realization and stay away from attainment, even the attainment of detachment, is named the general nature and form of emptiness in great vehicle."

Maitreya Bodhisattva asked the Buddha again, "World-Honored One, how many kinds of superior samadhi are absorbed in samatha and vipasyana?"

The Buddha replied to Maitreya Bodhisattva, "Good gentleman, as I have said, innumerable voice-hearers, bodhisattvas, and Thus-Comers have innumerable kinds of superior samadhi, and all of them are absorbed in samatha and vipasyana."

"World-Honored One, what are the causes of samatha and vipasyana?"

"Good gentleman, pure precepts and the correct views produced by pure hearing and thinking are the causes of samatha and vipasyana."

"World-Honored One, what are the effects of samatha and vipasyana?"

"Good gentleman, the virtuous pure mind and virtuous pure wisdom are the effects of samatha and vipasyana. Furthermore, good gentleman, all virtuous dharmas of voice-hearers and Thus-Comers in and beyond the world are the effects of samatha and vipasyana."

"World-Honored One, what is the karma of samatha and vipasyana?"

"Good gentleman, the karma of samatha and vipasyana is to get rid of two bondages: the bondage of deluded images and the bondage of heavy vexations."

"World-Honored One, the Buddha has taught that there are five bonds. Of them which will hinder samatha? Which will hinder vipasyana? And which will hinder both?"

"Good gentleman, attachment to body and property will hinder samatha. Inability and unwillingness to follow holy teachings will hinder vipasyana. Indulging in images, dwelling in impurity, and being easily satisfied with minor achievement will hinder both. Because of the first hindrance, the practitioners are unable to initiate cultivation. Because of the second hindrance, the practitioners are unable to put additional efforts to fulfill cultivation."

"World-Honored One, which of the five coverings will hinder samatha? Which will hinder vipasyana? And which will hinder both?"

"Good gentleman, restless mind and repentance will hinder samatha. Dullness, sleepiness, and doubt will hinder vipasyana. Greed and anger will hinder both."

"World-Honored One, how can we tell that someone has fulfilled perfect and pure samatha path?"

"Good gentleman, the practitioners will not be able to fulfill samatha path until they have not only correctly and completely eliminated restless mind and repentance, but also dullness, sleepiness, and doubt."

"World-Honored One, how can we tell that someone has fulfilled perfect and pure vipasyana path?"

"Good gentleman, the practitioners will not be able to fulfill vipasyana path until they have not only correctly and completely eliminated dullness, sleepiness, and doubt, but also restless mind and repentance."

"World-Honored One, how many kinds of distracted and restless mind of which the bodhisattvas should be aware when staying in samatha and vipasyana?"

"Good gentleman, there are five kinds of distracted and restless mind of which the bodhisattvas should be aware. They are intention instability, outer instability, inner instability, phenomena instability, and heavy-bondage instability. Good gentleman, if the bodhisattvas stay away from the aspiration to great vehicle but turn to the vehicle of voice-hearer and self-enlightened one, they are having intention instability. If they let their minds flow without least restraint in disorderly mess of images, thoughts, and associated vexations caused by five desires and related conditions, they are having outer instability. If they are in dullness and sleepiness so their minds are sinking, or they are fond of and attached to samapatti, or they are contaminated by vexations in samapatti, they are having inner instability. If they deliberately reflect on the images in samadhi caused by outer phenomena, they are having instability of phenomena. If they intend to give rise to various feelings, and their heavy vexations also activate ego and arrogance, they are having heavy-bondage instability."

"World-Honored One, what hindrances will samatha and vipasyana deal with in each of the stages from the first bodhisattva stage through the stage of Thus-Comer?"

"Good gentleman, in the first bodhisattva stage, samatha and vipasyana can deal with the contaminated hindrances of vexation, karma, and arising in inferior destinies. In the second bodhisattva stage, samatha and vipasyana can deal with the present hindrances caused by minor and subtle errors. In the third bodhisattva stage, they can deal with the hindrances caused by greedy desires. In the fourth bodhisattva stage, they can deal with the hindrances caused by the fondness of concentration and fondness of dharma. In the fifth bodhisattva stage, they can deal with the hindrances caused by earnest avoidance of birth and death and earnest aspiration to nirvana. In the sixth bodhisattva stage, they can deal with the hindrances caused by many present images. In the seventh bodhisattva stage, they can deal with the hindrances caused by the present minute images. In the eighth bodhisattva stage, they can deal with the hindrances caused by deliberate effort to achieve formlessness and by the uneasiness with form. In the ninth bodhisattva stage, they can deal with the hindrances caused by the uneasiness with all kinds of expedient and skillful speech. In the tenth bodhisattva stage, they can deal with the hindrances caused by the inability to realize the dharma body. Good gentleman, in the stage of Thus-Comer, samatha and vipasyana can deal with the subtlest hindrances of extremely minute vexations and knowledge. Once these hindrances are permanently terminated, the bodhisattvas will realize and attain all kinds of perfect knowledge and correct views without attachment and hesitation. After fulfilling what they have done, they are able to establish the purest dharma body."

Maitreya Bodhisattva asked the Buddha again, "World-Honored One, how do the bodhisattvas cultivate diligently based on samatha and vipasyana to realize and attain anuttara-samyak-sambodhi?"

The Buddha replied to Maiatreya Bodhisattva, "Good gentleman, when attaining samatha and vipasyana, the bodhisattvas will reflect correctly, based on the seven kinds of realness and with superior concentrative mind, on the well-examined, well-measured, and well-established nature of realness of what they have heard and thought. Because they can correctly reflect on realness this way, they are able to discard the very minute and subtle images, not to mention the coarse ones.

"Good gentleman, the so-called minute and subtle images are ones that our minds receive and hold. For instance, the images caused by reception and perception; the contaminated and purified images; the inner and outer images; the images caused by thinking that I should cultivate to benefit sentient beings; the images of correct knowledge, realness, the four noble truths, the conditioned dharmas, and the unconditioned dharmas; the images of permanence, impermanence, changes, and changelessness; the images of the sameness and differences of the conditioned dharmas; the images of knowing that all dharmas are always as they have been; the images of selfless individual sentient beings and the images of selfless dharmas. Because the images arise so often, we should deal with the bonds, coverings, and restlessness of our minds well constantly in order to discard them.

"From that time on, each of the seven kinds of realness will allow one to give rise to seven kinds of thorough knowledge from within. This is named seeing the path of the truth. When achieving this, the practitioners are named entering onto the bodhisattva path of nonarising. They are now reborn as a family member of the Thus-Comer and realize the first stage. They thus will benefit from the superior merits and virtues of this stage. They have by that time acquired two kinds of perceived objects, one with differentiated images and the other without differentiated images, owing to the attainment of samatha and vipasyana. Now because they have seen the path, they will acquire the third kind of perceived object: the one with the characteristics of all dharmas. At this moment they are ready to progress to higher stages and continue to investigate these three kinds of objects. Like taking out a thick wedge with a thinner one, the bodhisattvas will remove heavy defiled images by means of removing inner images. Upon removing all images, the heavy vexations will permanently extinguish. As progressing through the higher stages in later times, they will forge their minds like forging gold, and keep moving forward until realizing and attaining anuttara-samyak-sambodhi when they have fulfilled all necessary practices. Good gentleman, this is how the bodhisattvas realize and attain anuttara-samyak-sambodhi through the correct inner cultivation of concentration and investigation."

Maitreya Bodhisattva asked the Buddha again, "World-

Honored One, how will the practitioners elicit the far-reaching, broad, great, and powerful authority and virtues of bodhisattva?"

"Good gentleman, if the bodhisattvas know six spheres well, they will be able to elicit the far-reaching, broad, great, and powerful authority and virtues of bodhisattva. The first is to know well how the mind arises. The second is to know well how the mind dwells. The third is to know well how the mind gets away. The fourth is to know well how the mind increases. The fifth is to know well how the mind decreases. The sixth is to know expediency well.

"To know well how the mind arises means to know the sixteen different ways of mind arising as they really are.

"The first is the arising of the unintelligible, firm, and solid container of consciousness named adana consciousness.

"The second is the arising of various mental images caused by perceiving the objects. The conscious will either perceive instantly the physical objects, and the inner and outer feelings, or grasp many visions of concentrations, Buddha lands, and Thus-Comers, instantaneously.

"The third is the arising of minor images of particular beings caused by the consciousness connected with the realm of desire.

"The fourth is the arising of major images caused by the consciousness connected with the realm of form.

"The fifth is the arising of innumerable images caused by the spheres of boundless emptiness and boundless consciousness.

"The sixth is the arising of minute and subtle images caused by the sphere of nothingness.

"The seventh is the arising of images expanding to the

farthest edge caused by the sphere of nonthinking and not nonthinking.

"The eighth is the arising of formlessness caused by the consciousness of transcending the world and extinguishing conditions.

"The ninth is the arising of suffering caused by the consciousness connected with the hells.

"The tenth is the arising of mixed feelings caused by the consciousness connected with desires.

"The eleventh is the arising of joys caused by the consciousness connected with the first and second meditations.

"The twelfth is the arising of pleasures caused by the consciousness connected with the third meditation.

"The thirteenth is the arising of neither pains nor pleasures caused by the consciousness connected with the fourth meditation, fifth meditation, and so forth, and the concentration of nonthinking and not nonthinking.

"The fourteenth is the arising of contaminated images caused by the consciousness correspondent with major and subordinate vexations.

"The fifteenth is the arising of virtuous images caused by the consciousness correspondent with belief, no greed, no hatred, no harm, and so forth.

"The sixteenth is the arising of neutral images caused by the consciousness correspondent neither with the virtuous dharmas nor with the not virtuous dharmas.

"What does it mean to know well how the mind dwells? It means to really know the realness of perception. What does it mean to know well how the mind gets away? It means to really know how to get away from two kinds of bondage: the bondage of deluded images and the bondage of heavy vexations. What does it mean to know well how the mind increases? It means that as the two bondages accumulate and increase, the determination and power of the mind to get rid of them will increase accordingly. What does it mean to know well how the mind decreases? It means that as the two bondages diminish, the determination and power of the mind to get rid of them will decrease accordingly. What does it mean to know expediency well? It means to really know the superior merits of the eight liberations, eight vexation-overcoming meditations, and ten universal contemplations and decide to cultivate the desirable factors and cast off the undesirable elements expediently and skillfully. Good gentleman, this is how the bodhisattvas elicited, are eliciting, and will elicit the far-reaching, broad, and great authority, merits, and virtues of bodhisattva."

Maitreya Bodhisattva asked the Buddha again, "World-Honored One, you have taught that in nirvana without remainder all feelings cease permanently. What are these feelings?"

"Good gentleman, in summary there are two kinds of feelings that will cease permanently in the nirvana without remainder. What are they? They are the heavy feelings caused by body and the feelings caused by living environment. There are four kinds of heavy feelings caused by body: the vexations caused by the physical body; the feelings caused by the mind; the feelings caused by mature effects; and the feelings caused by immature effects. If the effects are mature, the karma makers have to receive the retribution now. If the effects are not mature yet, the retribution will appear in the future.

"There are also four kinds of feeling caused by living environment: the feelings derived from the world on which we rely; the feelings derived from living supplies; the feelings derived from using living supplies; and the feelings caused by attachment and grasping.

"In the nirvana with remainder, the practitioners have dealt with vexations well; they have gotten rid of ignorance and their feelings are purified because of the bright wisdom gained by them even though their karmic effects are not mature. They look as if they still had the same feelings as ordinary people, their feelings already become pure and flawless, not to mention the ones whose karmic effects are mature and who have ceased the heavy feelings caused by body and living environment. In the nirvana without remainder, all feelings cease permanently."

After saying these words to Maitreya Bodhisattva, the World-Honored One added, "Good gentleman, it is excellent that you could ask Thus-Comer questions about the most exquisite and purest yoga path. You have also attained the definitive and most expedient and skillful yoga. I am teaching you this perfect, purest, and most exquisite yoga path as all perfectly and universally enlightened ones had taught in the past and will teach in the future. Good gentlemen and gentlewomen, you should follow this path to cultivate and learn diligently and bravely."

At that time, the World-Honored One reiterated the same meanings in verse:

In the provisionally established dharma of yoga,

Those without self-restraint will lose great justice.
If they can rely on this dharma and yoga,
They will cultivate correctly and attain great enlightenment.

It seems right to seek in order to gain something,
But those who embrace this view will
As you know, Maitreya, stay far away from yoga.
It is just as remote as the vast land from sky.

How can you ignore the things really good for sentient beings?
Please be awake and cultivate diligently to benefit them.
The wise doing this for numberless kalpas,
Will attain the uppermost joy free from defilements.

Teaching the virtue of renunciation for self-interest,
Is demonstrating greed instead of giving.
Without knowing they own invaluable treasures,
The ignorant ones are wandering and searching as beggars.

Don't be attached to noisy and nonsensical arguments,
You should rather rise up to start superior diligence.
In order to deliver heavenly and human beings,
Yoga is just what you should learn.

At that time, Maitreya Bodhisattva asked the Buddha again, "World-Honored One, what is the name of this dharma gate of explicating the profound secret? How should we learn and practice this dharma gate?"

The Buddha replied to Maitreya Bodhisattva, "Good gentleman, this is named the teaching of the ultimate meaning of yoga. You should learn and practice this teaching of the ultimate meaning of yoga."

When the Buddha was teaching the ultimate meaning of yoga, six hundred thousand sentient beings in the assembly were inspired and determined to aspire to anuttara-samyak-sambodhi; three hundred thousand voice-hearers stayed far away from defilements and attained the pure dharma eye; one hundred fifty thousand voice-hearers removed all flaws and attained liberation; and seventy-five thousand bodhisattvas initiated broad and great aspiration for learning and practicing yoga.

The Ultimate Meaning of the Stages of Paramita

At that time, Viewing-in-Freedom Bodhisattva asked the Buddha, "World-Honored One, you have said that there are ten stages of bodhisattva. They are the stages of ecstasy, freedom from defilements, emitting light, flaming wisdom, being extremely difficult to be surpassed, realness manifestation, going far away, the unmovable, expedient wisdom, and dharma cloud. You have also said that the eleventh stage is the stage of Buddhahood. In what kinds of purity are these stages contained? In what levels are these stages absorbed?"

The World-Honored One replied to Viewing-in-Freedom Bodhisattva, "Good gentleman, you must know that the ten stages are absorbed in four kinds of purity and eleven levels. What are the four kinds of purity that absorb various stages? The increased purity of joyful intention absorbs the first stage. The increased purity of observing precept absorbs the second stage. The increased purity of mind absorbs the third stage. The increased purity of wisdom absorbs the fourth stage through the stage of Buddhahood, and this purity of wisdom will become more and more superior and exquisite as practitioners progress to the next higher stage. Good gentleman, you must know that these four kinds of purity absorb all stages.

"How do the eleven levels absorb all stages? First in the state of definitive-understanding actions, the bodhisattvas have cultivated and learned the definitive-understanding forbearance through ten ways very well. They then transcend this state and enter onto the bodhisattva path of nonarising.

"Because of this cause and condition, the bodhisattvas are able to fulfill the first level. But they still may commit minor faults and cannot act fully in accord with correct knowledge, therefore they need to cultivate and learn diligently and attentively in order to improve themselves.

"Because of the further cultivation and learning, the bodhisattvas are able to fulfill the second level. But they have not fulfilled the worldly samadhi, samapatti, and the dharani of hearing and retention, they need to cultivate and learn diligently and attentively in order to improve themselves.

"Because of their effort, the bodhisattvas are able to fulfill the third level. But they have neither learned and cultivated much, therefore they cannot dwell in the correct mindfulness of the factors for enlightenment, nor become free from the craving for samapatti and dharmas. They need to cultivate diligently and attentively in order to improve themselves.

"Because of their effort, the bodhisattvas are able to fulfill the fourth level. But they still cannot contemplate and investigate the truths as they really are, or renounce the intention of aspiring to nirvana and turning back from birth and death. They have not developed the expedient factors for the bodhi, therefore they need to cultivate and learn diligently and attentively in order to improve themselves.

"Because of their effort, the bodhisattvas are able to fulfill the fifth level. But they still cannot fully contemplate and investigate the reality of drifting in birth and death as it really is, they thus become disgusted with the drifting and cannot dwell in formlessness much, therefore they need to cultivate and learn diligently and attentively in order to improve themselves.

"Because of their effort, the bodhisattvas are able to fulfill the sixth level. But they have not cultivated and learned much enough to dwell in formlessness incessantly and flawlessly, they need to cultivate and learn diligently and attentively in order to improve themselves.

"Because of their effort, the bodhisattvas now are able to fulfill the seventh level. But because they still cannot dwell in formlessness free from deliberate effort, nor can they feel free and comfortable in form, they need to cultivate and learn diligently and attentively in order to improve themselves.

"Because of their effort, the bodhisattvas now are able to fulfill the eighth level. But they still cannot teach freely and at ease the differences of various names, forms, and interpretations of all kinds of dharmas, so they need to cultivate and learn diligently and attentively in order to improve themselves.

"Because of their effort, the bodhisattvas now are able to fulfill the ninth level. But they have not fully realized the dharma body presently, so they need to cultivate and learn diligently and attentively in order to improve themselves.

"Because of their effort, the bodhisattvas are able to fulfill the tenth level. But they have not attained exquisite wisdom and views free from hindrance and attachment in all kinds of knowledge, therefore they need further to cultivate and learn diligently and attentively in order to overcome this weakness. Once they have successfully fulfilled this level, they will also fulfill all levels. Good gentleman, this is how all these eleven levels can absorb various stages."

Viewing-in-Freedom Bodhisattva asked the Buddha again, "World-Honored One, why is the first stage named the stage of ecstasy? Why are the second, third, and so forth and the tenth stages named the stage of freedom from defilements, the stage of emitting light, and so forth? Why is the highest level named the stage of Buddhahood?"

The Buddha replied to Viewing-in-Freedom Bodhisattva, "Good gentleman, when the practitioners attain superior understanding of the truth and develop a mind beyond the world that they have never had before and thus experience a great joy, they are entering the first stage of ecstasy. When the practitioners stay far away from all kinds of minor and subtle violation of precepts, they are entering the second stage of freedom from defilements.

"Because the samadhi and the dharani of hearing and retention that the practitioners have attained can serve as the basis for the unlimited light of intelligence, they are named entering the third stage of emitting light. After attaining the factors for enlightenment, they have burned all vexations up and are named entering the fourth stage of flaming wisdom. After cultivating and learning the factors for enlightenment expediently through an extremely difficult process, they have finally attained self-ease and are named achieving the fifth stage of being extremely difficult to be surpassed.

"Because the practitioners have deliberately focused on the cultivation of formlessness in contemplating the drifting phenomena present in front of them, they are entering the sixth stage of realness manifestation. Because the practitioners have realized the flawless, uninterrupted, and formless intentions closely connected with the faraway pure lands, they are entering the seventh stage of going far away. Because of attaining effortless formlessness, the practitioners are no more moved by the vexations arising presently, so they are named entering the eighth stage of the unmovable.

"As the practitioners attain broad and great unhindered knowledge and wisdom, and feel comfortable and at ease for giving lectures on all kinds of dharma, they are named entering the ninth stage of expedient wisdom. As the practitioners feel that their heavy bodies have expanded as vast empty space and the dharma body has become a huge cloud covering everything, they are named entering the tenth stage of dharma cloud. As the bodhisattvas can permanently eliminate the extremely minute and subtle vexations and the hindrances caused by knowledge, get rid of attachment and obstacles, and attain the perfect and universal enlightenment in all kinds of knowledge, they are named entering the eleventh stage of Buddhahood."

Viewing-in-Freedom Bodhisattva asked the Buddha again, "How many kinds of ignorance and heavy bondages should be dealt with in these stages?"

The Buddha replied to Viewing-in-Freedom Bodhisattva, "Good gentleman, twenty-two kinds of ignorance and eleven kinds of heavy bondages should be dealt with in all these stages. In the first stage, the ignorance insisting that individual sentient beings and all dharmas are real and the ignorance related to the contaminated dharmas in inferior destinies along with their heavy bondages should be dealt with.

"In the second stage, the ignorance in regard to minor and subtle mistakes unintentionally made and the ignorance related to various karmic destinies along with their heavy bondages should be dealt with.

"In the third stage, the ignorance in regard to greedy desire and the ignorance for fulfilling the dharani of hearing and retention along with their heavy bondages should be dealt with.

"In the four stage, the ignorance in craving for samapatti and the ignorance in craving for the dharma along with their heavy bondages should be dealt with.

"In the fifth stage, the ignorance of persistent deliberate intention to avoid birth and death and the ignorance of persistent deliberate intention to approach nirvana along with their heavy bondages should be dealt with.

"In the sixth stage, the ignorance in contemplating the phenomena of drifting and the ignorance caused by many images appearing presently along with their heavy bondages should be dealt with.

"In the seventh stage, the ignorance in realizing the very minute and subtle images and the ignorance of continuously paying deliberate and expedient attention to formlessness along with their heavy bondages should be dealt with.

"In the eighth stage, the ignorance of contemplating formlessness with deliberate effort and the inability of mastering images freely and at ease along with their heavy bondages should be dealt with.

"In the ninth stage, the inability to attain unhindered understanding of innumerable words and sentences, unhindered understanding of meanings, unhindered teaching, and unhindered talent of debate along with their heavy bondages should be dealt with.

"In the tenth stage, the inability to play great supernatural powers and the inability to realize the extremely subtle and profound secret along with their heavy bondages should be dealt with.

"In the stage of Thus-Comer, the extremely subtle attachment to images and the extremely subtle hindrance of knowledge along with their heavy bondages should be dealt with.

"Good gentleman, in order to deal with these twenty-two kinds of ignorance and eleven heavy bondages, all these stages are established. Anuttara-samyak-sambodhi (the unsurpassed, perfect, and universal bodhi) exactly signifies the perfect liberation from the heavy bondages."

Viewing-in-Freedom Bodhisattva said to the Buddha again, "World-Honored One, anuttara-samyak-sambodhi is very rare and unique! It can bestow such great benefits and positive effects on bodhisattvas so that they are able to break through the huge network of ignorance and puzzles, cross the heavy, thick, and dark forests, and realize and attain the unsurpassed bodhi presently."

Viewing-in-Freedom Bodhisattva further asked the Buddha, "World-Honored One, how many superior things have well established these stages?"

The Buddha replied to Viewing-in-Freedom Bodhisattva, "Good gentleman, eight superior things have well established these stages. The first is the purity of highly motivated joyful intention. The second is the purity of mind. The third is the purity of compassion. The fourth is the purity of ferrying over to the other shore. The fifth is the purity of seeing, making offerings respectfully to, and offering services to the Buddhas. The sixth is the purity of assisting sentient beings to mature. The seventh is the purity of arising. The eighth is the purity of authority and virtues.

"Good gentleman, all these kinds of purity, including the purity of the highly motivated joyful intention, the purity of mind, and so forth, and the purity of authority and virtues will become more superior as practitioners progress from the first stage through the rest of stages except in the stage of Buddhahood where the purity of arising is not existent. All merits and virtues included in the first stage will also appear in the rest of stages although each stage has its particular superior merits and virtues. None of these ten stages is unsurpassed. Only the merits and virtues of the stage of Buddhahood are unsurpassed."

Viewing-in-Freedom Bodhisattva asked the Buddha again, "World-Honored One, why is it said that the birth of bodhisattva is the most unique and superior one among all kinds of birth?"

The Buddha replied to Viewing-in-Freedom Bodhisattva, "Good gentleman, it is based on four reasons. The first is that the birth of bodhisattva results from the accumulation of the extremely pure virtuous roots. The second is that the birth of bodhisattva is out of their intelligent choices. The third is that the birth of bodhisattva is caused by merciful and compassionate vows to delivering all sentient beings. The fourth is that only if the bodhisattvas have purified themselves can they purify others."

Viewing-in-Freedom Bodhisattva asked the Buddha again, "World-Honored One, why is it said that the bodhisattvas are doing their jobs with great, broad, exquisite, and superior aspirations?"

The Buddha replied, "Good gentleman, it is because of four reasons. The first is that the bodhisattvas understand nirvana very well and love to reside in it. The second is that they are able to realize and attain it quickly. The third is that they can further relieve themselves from being attached to and dwelling in it. The fourth is that they vow to suffer endlessly in order to benefit various sentient beings without conditions and differentiation. That is why I say that these bodhisattvas have great, broad, exquisite, and superior aspirations."

Viewing-in-Freedom Bodhisattva asked the Buddha again, "World-Honored One, what are the areas of learning that the bodhisattvas should learn?"

The Buddha replied to Viewing-in-Freedom Bodhisattva, "Good gentleman, briefly speaking, there are six areas of learning that the bodhisattvas should learn: giving, precept, forbearance, diligence, meditation, and wisdom (prajna) leading to the other shore."

Viewing-in-Freedom Bodhisattva asked the Buddha again, "World-Honored One, among these six areas, which are contained in the superior precept? Which are contained in the superior concentration of mind? And which are contained in the superior wisdom?"

The Buddha replied to Viewing-in-Freedom Bodhisattva, "Good gentleman, the first three areas, namely, giving, precept, and forbearance, are contained in the superior precept. Meditation is contained in the superior concentration of mind. Prajna is contained in the superior wisdom. I will say that diligence is contained in all of them."

Viewing-in-Freedom Bodhisattva asked the Buddha again, "World-Honored One, among these six areas of learning, which areas will serve to nurture bliss and virtues, and which will serve to nurture prajna?"

The Buddha replied to Viewing-in-Freedom Bodhisattva, "Good gentleman, what absorbed in superior precept will serve to nurture bliss and virtues; what absorbed in superior wisdom will serve to nurture prajna; while diligence and meditation will serve to nurture all."

Viewing-in-Freedom Bodhisattva asked the Buddha again, "World-Honored One, how should the bodhisattvas cultivate and learn these six things?"

The Buddha replied to Viewing-in-Freedom Bodhisattva, "Good gentleman, five approaches should be adopted by the bodhisattvas. The first is to believe bravely and understand sharply the exquisite and subtle correct teachings of bodhisattva-path texts correspondent with paramita. The second is to cultivate diligently the ten dharma actions with the exquisite knowledge developed and formed through hearing, reflection, and cultivation. The third is to protect the bodhi mind at all times. The fourth is to keep close connections with the real, virtuous intellectuals. The fifth is to practice the virtuous dharmas arduously and incessantly."

Viewing-in-Freedom Bodhisattva asked the Buddha again, "World-Honored One, why are only these six areas of learning established particularly for the bodhisattvas?"

The Buddha replied to Viewing-in-Freedom Bodhisat-tva, "Good gentleman, there are two reasons. One is that these six areas of learning will benefit all sentient beings. The other is that they will serve to overcome and eliminate various vexations. The first three kinds of learning will benefit all sentient beings; the latter three ones will eliminate vexations. The bodhisattvas will give living supplies so as to satisfy the needs of the sentient beings. Because of observing pure precept, the bodhisattvas will not oppress, annoy, or do harm to sentient beings. They will rather always do things beneficial for them. Because of forbearance, the bodhisattvas will tolerate damages, disturbances, insults, and pressures put on them by the sentient beings, nor will they turn away from the sentient beings. This is how the first three things will benefit sentient beings. The latter three things will assist the bodhisattvas to deal with their own vexations. Because of diligence, the bodhisattvas are able to cultivate virtuous actions bravely and constantly. Although for the time being they cannot remove vexations and the hidden negative roots permanently, they will not be at least hindered by the remained afflictions in additional efforts of cultivating virtuous dharmas. Because of meditation, they will be able to remove all vexations permanently. Because of prajna, the bodhisattvas will be able to eliminate all hidden roots of vexations forever."

Viewing-in-Freedom Bodhisattva asked the Buddha again, "World-Honored One, why are the four more paramitas established for the bodhisattvas?"

The Buddha replied to Viewing-in-Freedom Bodhisattva, "Good gentleman, it is because these four paramitas will assist the six paramitas. When absorbing the sentient beings with the first three of the six paramitas, the bodhisattvas need expedient skills so as to let the sentient beings reside in virtues. That is why I have established expedient skillfulness paramita as an aid to the first three paramitas.

"Some bodhisattvas have too many vexations in present life

to cultivate the incessant intuitive contemplation. Some bodhisattvas have inferior intentions. They love the realm of desire and attain more definitive understanding of this realm than other realms, so they cannot dwell in inner peace. Some bodhisattvas do not have good chances to hear the texts of bodhisattva path, their meditations cannot elicit the wisdom beyond the world, so they can only absorb little bliss and virtues. In order to diminish their vexations in future life, they need to initiate correct aspiration. That is why aspiration paramita is established. Because of this aspiration, the bodhisattvas will have less vexations in the lives to come so will be able to cultivate more diligently. That is why I have established aspiration paramita as an aid to diligence paramita."

"If the bodhisattvas can stay close to virtuous persons, listen to correct dharma, and reflect reasonably, their inferior intentions will become superior, so they will attain definitive understanding of the realm of form and the realm of formlessness. This is named power paramita. Because of this power, their minds will dwell in peace. That is why I have taught power paramita as an aid to meditation paramita.

"If the bodhisattvas have good access to the texts of bodhisattva path, listen to, and cultivate and learn them, then they will elicit the practice of meditation. This is named intelligence paramita. Because of this intelligence, the bodhisattvas are able to elicit the wisdom beyond the world. That is why I have taught intelligence paramita as an aid to wisdom paramita."

Viewing-in-Freedom Bodhisattva asked the Buddha again, "World-Honored One, why is the teaching of the six paramitas arranged in this particular order?"

The Buddha replied to Viewing-in-Freedom Bodhisattva,

"Good gentleman, it is because in this order each paramita will serve to initiate the next one. If the bodhisattvas are no more attached to their bodies and personal properties, they are ready to accept pure precept. In order to protect pure precept, they will have to cultivate forbearance. After cultivating forbearance, they will further initiate diligence. After becoming diligent, they will further practice meditation. The practice of meditation will lead one to the attainment of the wisdom beyond the world. That is why I have taught the paramitas in this particular order."

Viewing-in-Freedom Bodhisattva asked the Buddha again, "World-Honored One, how many different kinds of practice are included in each of the six paramitas?"

The Buddha replied to Viewing-in-Freedom Bodhisattva, "Good gentleman, there are three kinds of practice in each paramita. The three kinds of giving are dharma giving, property giving, and fearlessness giving. The three kinds of pure precept are observing precept to discard negative actions, observing precept to generate positive actions, and observing precept to benefit all sentient beings. The three kinds of forbearance are responding to resentment and the harm caused by others with patience but without hatred, accepting suffering with peaceful mind, and contemplating and realizing dharma forbearance. The three kinds of diligence are moving forward diligently by wearing armors, generating virtuous dharmas with additional efforts, and working with additional efforts to benefit sentient beings. The three kinds of meditation are the meditation for dwelling in tranquil nondifferentiation and extremely tranquil guiltlessness for dealing with vexations, pleasures, and pains; the meditation for eliciting merits and virtues; and the meditation for benefiting sentient beings. The three kinds of wisdom are the worldly wisdom, the superior ultimate wisdom, and the wisdom beneficial for sentient beings.

Viewing-in-Freedom Bodhisattva asked the Buddha again, "World-Honored One, why is paramita named paramita?"

The Buddha replied to Viewing-in-Freedom Bodhisattva, "Good gentleman, it is based on five reasons: paramita is without defiled attachment; paramita is without craving; paramita is without wrongdoing; paramita is without differentiation; and paramita always transfers merits and virtues correctly. Being without defiled attachment means that paramita is not attached to the things contrary to paramita. Being without craving means that paramita is not bound by the effects that mature in different ways and at different times, nor does it expect anything in return. Being without wrongdoing means that it is not mixed and contaminated, nor does it stay away from expediency. Being without differentiation means that it is not attached to the particular characteristics of the dharmas as the languages do. Transferring merits and virtues correctly means that it will transfer all merits and virtues accumulated toward the unsurpassed great bodhi."

"World-Honored One, what are the things contrary to paramita?"

"Good gentleman, you must know that six things are contrary to paramita. The first is to view the desires for joys, pleasures, wealth, and self-ease as merits, virtues, and superior benefits. The second is to view indulging in the present pleasures of body, speech, and mind without self-restraint as merits, virtues, and superior benefits. The third is to view intolerance for contempt and insults as merits, virtues, and superior benefits. The fourth is to view laziness and satisfaction of desires as merits, virtues, and superior benefits. The fifth is to view the chaos in disorderly world as merits, virtues, and superior benefits. The sixth is to view seeing, hearing, and knowing the nonsensical arguments as merits, virtues, and superior benefits."

"World-Honored One, what effects that mature in different ways and at different times will result from the practice of all paramitas?"

"Good gentleman, there are six effects. The first is gaining great fortune. The second is being reborn in good destinies. The third is inviting no complaints or harm but various kinds of joy and happiness. The fourth is becoming a leader of sentient beings. The fifth is having no physical pains or diseases. The sixth is forming a great lineage of learning."

"World-Honored One, what are the paramitas mixed with contaminated dharmas?"

"Good gentleman, the contaminated dharmas are produced because of four additional efforts. The first is the additional effort without compassion. The second is the unreasonable additional effort. The third is the inconstant additional effort. The fourth is the additional effort without sincerity and dignity. The unreasonable effort means that when cultivating one paramita, the bodhisattvas will stay far away from, lose, or destroy the rest of paramitas."

"World-Honored One, what is the inexpedient action?"

"Good gentleman, the inexpedient action means that when practicing paramita to benefit sentient beings, the bodhisattvas are satisfied with merely giving them money and physical materials but neglect to teach them how to stay away from the not virtuous and turn to the virtuous actions. Why? Good gentleman, offering money or physical materials alone is not really beneficial to the sentient beings. It is like that one cannot turn animal droppings into clean and aromatic objects whether they are many or not. If the sentient beings choose negative ways, they will inevitably experience the suffering of life. Money or physical materials can only sooth people temporarily but cannot really solve their problems unless an expedient and appropriate approach is adopted. The real best benefits come from establishing sentient beings in exquisite and virtuous dharmas."

Viewing-in-Freedom Bodhisattva asked the Buddha again, "World-Honored One, how many kinds of purity are there in all paramitas?"

The Buddha replied to Viewing-in-Freedom Bodhisattva, "Good gentleman, I do not think there is any kind of purity that is not contained in the five reasons mentioned above. But now I would like to further elaborate from both general and particular perspectives. From the general perspective, there are seven forms of purity in practicing paramitas. The first is that when practicing paramitas, the bodhisattvas are not concerned whether others know them or not. The second is that when seeing and knowing the paramitas, the bodhisattvas will not be attached to them. The third is that the bodhisattvas are not skeptical or puzzled when practicing paramitas, so they will not ask this question: Can I attain the great bodhi? The fourth is that the bodhisattvas do not boast about themselves, slander others, or look down on others. The fifth is that the bodhisattvas are neither arrogant nor lacking self-restraint. The sixth is that the bodhisattvas are not satisfied with minor achievements. The seventh is that the bodhisattvas will not become jealous and stingy because of practicing the paramitas.

"From the particular perspective, there are also seven forms of purity for each paramita. The bodhisattvas should follow the seven forms of pure giving in cultivation as I have taught. They will practice pure giving by giving pure things. They will practice pure giving by observing pure precepts. They will practice pure giving with pure views. They will practice pure giving with pure minds. They will practice pure giving by speaking pure words. They will practice pure giving based on pure wisdom. They will practice pure giving by purifying defilements. These are the seven forms of pure giving.

"Furthermore, the bodhisattvas will learn to know well how all precepts, laws, demeanors, and rituals are established. They will know well the proper way to repent when violating precepts. They will observe precepts constantly. They will dwell firmly in precepts. They will behave in accord with precepts at all times. They will learn to act in accord with precepts effortlessly. They will learn all kinds of precepts, rules, rituals, and laws. These are the seven forms of pure precept.

"The bodhisattvas deeply believe that one's karmic effects will finally mature at different times and in different ways; therefore, when undesirable things happen to them, they will not complain, get angry, scold back to, fight back to, threaten, or play tricks on others. They will not do harm to others. They will not stay in hatred. They will not offend others when giving advice. They will not let things get worse without trying to solve the problems or arguments beforehand. They will not keep silent only because they are threatened or out of greedy desire. They will not stop giving advice only because they have already done once. These are the seven pure forms of forbearance.

"The bodhisattvas will fully understand the nature of equality in practicing diligence. They do not exaggerate their own strengths or dispise others when practicing diligence brave-ly. They possess great power and authority. They move forward powerfully. They are capable of overcoming difficulties. They are resolute, brave, and vigorous. They will never stay away from virtuous dharmas. These are the seven pure forms of diligence.

"The bodhisattvas will master the images of samadhi well. They will fulfill the realness of samadhi. They will practice different kinds of samadhi, the worldly and the ultimate, si-multaneously. They will master samatha and vipasyana freely. They will practice the samadhi of emptiness, formlessness, and nonaspiration freely. They will cultivate the samadhi of eight liberations, eight vexation-overcoming meditations, nine con-centrations, and ten universal contemplations freely. They will cultivate and learn numberless samadhi based on hearing texts of bodhisattva path. These are the seven pure forms of medita-tion.

"If the bodhisattvas stay far away from the two extremes and walk on the middle path, they are named possessing wis-dom. Because of this wisdom, they will be able to realize the true meanings of the liberation gates of emptiness, formless-ness, and nonaspiration as they really are. They will realize the meanings of the three kinds of nature: the nature of universal attachment, the nature of dependent origination, and the na-ture of perfect realization as they really are; that is, their natures are without selfness. They will realize the meanings of the three kinds of selflessness: the selflessness of images, the selflessness of arising, and the selflessness of ultimate meaning as they really are. They will realize the meanings of the five kinds of the world-ly learning: language and literature, technology, medicine, logic, and inner learning (the religious, spiritual, and philosophical) as they really are. They will also realize the ultimate meanings, namely, the seven kinds of realness, as they really are. Because of nondifferentiation, staying away from nonsensical arguments, dwelling in pure unified essential meanings, and taking care of numberless general perspectives of the dharmas, and also because of vipasyana, the bodhisattvas are able to accomplish the cultivation in accord with correct dharma. These are the seven pure forms of wisdom."

Viewing-in-Freedom Bodhisattva asked the Buddha again, "World-Honored One, as mentioned above, paramita is named paramita because of five reasons or five causes and conditions. What are the operation effects of these five causes and conditions?"

The Buddha replied to Viewing-in-Freedom Bodhisattva, "Good gentleman, there are five effects caused by the five causes and conditions. Because the bodhisattvas are free from contamination and attachment, they can cultivate paramitas constantly, sincerely, and diligently in present life; they are neither lazy nor without restraint at all. Because they are free from craving, they will absorb the factors of self-restraint as the causes for the effects of cultivation in the future. Because they do not do anything wrong, they are able to cultivate and learn paramitas in an extremely perfect, pure, and virtuous way. Because they are without differentiation, they are able to fulfill expedient and skillful paramita quickly. Because of correct transference, they will enjoy paramitas and their desirable effects without exhaustion wherever they are reborn until attaining the unsurpassed, perfect, and universal bodhi."

Viewing-in-Freedom Bodhisattva asked the Buddha again, "World-Honored One, among all paramitas, which are the broadest ones? Which are the unpolluted ones? Which are the brightest and most prosperous ones? Which are the unmovable ones? And which are the purest ones?"

The Buddha replied to Viewing-in-Freedom Bodhisattva, "Good gentleman, the broadest paramitas are the ones with correct transference but without pollution, attachment, craving, and clinging. The brightest and most prosperous ones are those without wrongdoing and differentiation, but with unpolluted wise reflection and choice in actions. The unmovable ones are those entering the stage of nonregression. The paramitas absorbed in the tenth stage and the stage of Buddhahood are the purest ones."

Viewing-in-Freedom Bodhisattva asked the Buddha again, "Based on what cause and condition to say that because the desirable positive effects of paramita that mature at different times and in different ways gained by the bodhisattvas are usually unexhausted, so is the paramita?"

The Buddha replied to Viewing-in-Freedom Bodhisattva, "Good gentleman, it is because the desirable positive effects will turn into causes for the effects to come in the future and generate more practices and cultivations. This succession of causes and effects will continue uninterruptedly once it starts."

Viewing-in-Freedom Bodhisattva asked the Buddha again, "World-Honored One, based on what causes and conditions to say that the bodhisattvas believe in, enjoy, and treasure the paramita not merely because they can gain desirable positive effects that mature in different ways and at different times?"

The Buddha replied to Viewing-in-Freedom Bodhisattva, "Good gentleman, it is because of five reasons. The first is that paramita is a powerful cause to generate joy and pleasure. The second is that paramita can benefit oneself and others in the final analysis. The third is that paramita can bring about desirable and positive effects in the future. The fourth is that paramita can deal with and remove all defilements. The fifth is that paramita is indestructible in the final analysis because it will make perfect tranquility and peace of nirvana possible."

Viewing-in-Freedom Bodhisattva asked the Buddha again, "World-Honored One, what most superior authorities and virtues are there for all paramitas?"

The Buddha replied to Viewing-in-Freedom Bodhisattva, "Good gentleman, there are four most superior authorities and virtues for all paramitas. The first is that when correctly cultivating paramita, the bodhisattvas are able to discard stinginess, precept violation, hatred and anger, tiredness and laziness, restlessness, and incorrect views. The second is that when correctly cultivating paramitas, the bodhisattvas are able to prepare real nutrients for the attainment of the unsurpassed, perfect, and universal bodhi. The third is that when correctly cultivating the paramita, the bodhisattvas are able to learn much to benefit themselves in present life so as to benefit sentient beings. The fourth is that when correctly cultivating the paramita, the bodhisattvas are able to attain the broad and unexhausted desirable effects in the future."

Viewing-in-Freedom Bodhisattva asked the Buddha again, "World-Honored One, what are the cause, effect, and the justice and benefit of all paramitas?"

The Buddha replied to Viewing-in-Freedom Bodhisattva, "Good gentleman, great compassion is the cause of all paramitas. The exquisite, subtle, and desirable results beneficial for all sentient beings are the effects of all paramitas. The perfect, unsurpassed, broad, and great bodhi is the grand justice and benefit of all paramitas."

Viewing-in-Freedom Bodhisattva asked the Buddha again, "World-Honored One, as the bodhisattvas possess all kinds of unexhausted properties and treasures and also have great compassion, why are there so many poor sentient beings in the world?"

The Buddha replied to Viewing-in-Freedom Bodhisattva, "Good gentleman, it is because of the effects caused by the negative karmas made by the sentient beings. The bodhisattvas have sufficient properties and treasures and are willing to bring them to all sentient beings. If the sentient beings are not hindered by their own negative karmas, there will be no poverty in the world. The evil ghosts are always extremely thirsty. But when they see the ocean, the waters will immediately dry up. It is not the ocean's fault; it is because of the negative karmas made by the ghosts. The properties and treasures offered by the bodhisattvas are like the ocean. It is not the bodhisattvas' faults that the sentient beings cannot drink water; it is rather the negative karmas that make sentient beings themselves always in need of water."

Viewing-in-Freedom Bodhisattva asked the Buddha again, "World-Honored One, based on what paramita do the bodhisattvas adopt selflessness as the nature of all dharmas? World-Honored One, if prajna paramita can adopt selflessness as the nature of all dharmas, why does it not adopt selfness as the nature of all dharmas?"

"Good gentleman, I will not say that the selfless nature can adopt the selfless nature. The selfless nature is realized from within apart from all kinds of languages, but it cannot be expressed without speech and words. That is why I say that prajna paramita can adopt selflessness as the nature of all dharmas."

Viewing-in-Freedom Bodhisattva asked the Buddha again, "World-Honored One, as the Buddha has said, there are three kinds of paramita: paramita, near [great][1] paramita, and great paramita. What is the paramita? What is the near [great] paramita? What is the great paramita?"

The Buddha replied to Viewing-in-Freedom Bodhisattva, "Good gentleman, the bodhisattvas have cultivated giving, pure precept, and so forth for a long time. They have attained the virtuous dharmas but still cannot subjugate vexations. They are in the soft phase of definitive-understanding level and are ready to transit to the higher level, so they are named in paramita. As the bodhisattvas continue to cultivate giving and so forth and accomplish more virtuous dharmas, they will be able to overcome vexations instead of being subjugated by them although vexations still remain active. They have reached the first stage and above and are very close to the great paramita, so they are named near [great] paramita. If the bodhisattvas keep cultivating giving and so forth and accomplish more virtuous dharmas, and finally reach the eighth stage and above when all their vexations being removed, they are named achieving great paramita."

Viewing-in-Freedom Bodhisattva asked the Buddha again, "World-Honored One, how many kinds of hidden inherent seeds of vexations are there in various stages?"

The Buddha replied to Viewing-in-Freedom Bodhisattva, "Good gentleman, there are briefly three kinds of hidden inherent seeds of vexations. The first is named the vexations

---

1   The original Chinese translation does not have "great"; they are "paramita, near paramita, and great paramita." In order to make the writing more reasonable, the English translator inserted [great] here.

with no more activator. Why is it so named? It is because the non-inherent vexations always play the role of activating the inherent seeds of vexations. As these non-inherent vexations are removed permanently in the fifth stage, the activator of the inherent vexations will also be eliminated. Therefore it is named the vexations with no more activator. The second is the weak vexations that will be removed in the sixth and the seventh stages. The third is the very subtle vexations that will be removed in the eighth stage and above. From that time on, all vexations will never arise while the hindrance to perfect knowledge still remains."

Viewing-in-Freedom Bodhisattva asked the Buddha again, "World-Honored One, how is the removal of the hidden vexations manifested by the termination of heavy bondages?"

The Buddha replied to Viewing-in-Freedom Bodhisattva, "Good gentleman, the removal of the hidden vexations is manifested by the termination of two kinds of heavy bondages. The first is the termination of the heavy bondages in the outer layer of skin; this is manifested in the first and the second stages of bodhisattva cultivation. The second is the termination of the heavy bondages in the inner layer of skin; this is manifested in the third stage of bodhisattva cultivation. When the heavy bondages in the bone are terminated, all hidden roots of vexations will also be removed permanently; and this is in the stage of Buddhahood."

Viewing-in-Freedom Bodhisattva asked the Buddha again, "World-Honored One, how many kalpas will it take to terminate these heavy bondages?"

The Buddha replied to Viewing-in-Freedom Bodhisattva, "Good gentleman, it will take three great countless kalpas or numberless kalpas for terminating these heavy bondages. Namely, it will take as many kalpas as countless years, months, half months, days and nights, hours, half hours, brief instants, eye blinks and breaths, and ksanas."

Viewing-in-Freedom Bodhisattva asked the Buddha again, "World-Honored One, what are the forms as the vexations of various bodhisattvas arise in each stage? What will the bodhisattvas lose? What virtues will they gain?"

The Buddha replied to Viewing-in-Freedom Bodhisattva, "Good gentleman, the forms are without contamination. Why? As the bodhisattvas reach the first stage, they must have thoroughly known all dharma realms. Because of this reason, the bodhisattvas will be aware that their vexations are going to arise, the forms of the vexations thus are without contamination. Because they do not have suffering, they will lose nothing. When their vexations arise, the great bodhisattvas are able to benefit the sentient beings by ceasing the causes of their suffering, so they have innumerable merits and virtues."

Viewing-in-Freedom Bodhisattva said to the Buddha and acclaimed, "It is unusual, World-Honored One! The unsurpassed bodhi has such great virtues and benefits! It enables the bodhisattvas to become superior to the virtuous roots possessed by all sentient beings, voice-hearers, and self-enlightened ones even if they have vexations arise, not to mention they have other numberless merits and virtues."

Viewing-in-Freedom Bodhisattva asked the Buddha again, "World-Honored One, you have said that there is only one vehicle, but you have also mentioned the voice-hearer vehicle and the great vehicle. What secret meaning does this imply?"

The Buddha replied to Viewing-in-Freedom Bodhisattva, "Good gentleman, I have taught the particular natures of various dharmas in the voice-hearer vehicle, such as the five aggregates, six inner spheres, six outer spheres, and so forth. In the great vehicle I have also taught that all these dharmas share the same dharma realm and the same essential meaning. I do not teach the differences between the natures of these two vehicles. But some persons misunderstood my words owing to their deluded differentiation; they either added something to what I say or subtracted something from what I say, and suggested the meanings not implied by me. They even insisted that these vehicles were in conflict and argued against each other endlessly. This is the secret meaning implied by it."

At that time, the World-Honored One reiterated this meaning in verse:

> *In various stages, the ways for dealing with vexations are*
> *   contained,*
> *Superior aspirations and various kinds of learning are thus*
> *   initiated.*
> *To follow the Buddha's teachings is the great vehicle.*
> *Perfect cultivation of this vehicle will enable one greatly*
> *   enlightened.*

> *After teaching that the dharmas have different characteristics,*
> *I further remind you that they are all with one essential*
> *   meaning.*
> *No matter they are named inferior vehicle or superior vehicle,*
> *I won't say that they have different natures.*

Deluded differentiation in speaking about the meaning,
Will add something to or take something from my original
    saying.
When misguided views assert that two vehicles are in conflict,
The ignorant understanding will thus bring about controversy.

At that time, Viewing-in-Freedom Bodhisattva asked the Buddha again, "World-Honored One, what is the name of this profound and secret dharma gate? How should we accept and practice it?"

The Buddha replied to Viewing-in-Freedom Bodhisattva, "Good gentleman, this dharma gate is named the ultimate meaning of the stages of paramita. You should follow its meaning and cultivate it accordingly."

When the Buddha was teaching the ultimate meaning of the stages of paramita, seventy-five thousand bodhisattvas in the assembly attained the Great Vehicle Bright Samadhi of the bodhisattva.

The Things Fulfilled by the Thus-Comer

At that time, Manjusri Great Bodhisattva asked the Buddha, "World-Honored One, you have taught about the dharma body of the Thus-Comer. What is the dharma body of the Thus-Comer?"

The Buddha replied to Manjusri Bodhisattva, "Good gentleman, if ones have cultivated getting away well in various stages of paramita and fulfilled transformation, they are having dharma body. This dharma body is inconceivable for two reasons: It is without nonsensical arguments and without doing. On the contrary, the ordinary sentient beings care about and are attached to nonsensical arguments and always intend to do something."

"World-Honored One, do the voice-hearers and self-enlightened ones also attain dharma body after transformation?"

"No, good gentleman, it is not named dharma body."

"World-Honored One, then what is it named?'

"Good gentleman, it is named the liberation body instead. As in terms of liberation body, we may say that all voice-hearers and self-enlightened ones are not different from the Thus-Comers. But in terms of dharma body, their merits and virtues are much inferior to the Thus-Comers' by numberless times even beyond calculation and similes."

Manjusri Bodhisattva asked the Buddha again, "World-Honored One, how do we know that the Thus-Comer is arising?"

The Buddha replied to Manjusri Bodhisattva, "Good gentleman, the transformed bodies of all Thus-Comers operate like the arising of all species in the world. As we see the Thus-Comers are dwelling in the dignity and beauty of their merits and virtues as they have always been, we know that their transformed bodies do arise, but their dharma bodies never arise."

Manjusri Bodhisattva asked the Buddha again, "World-Honored One, how do the Thus-Comers demonstrate the arising of their transformed bodies in an expedient and skillful way?"

The Buddha replied to Manjusri Bodhisattva, "Good gentleman, in all Buddha lands of the large threefold thousand-world, the Thus-Comers entered human wombs and were reborn in a widely respected and admired king's family or tremendously blessed family, in which they grew up, lived a family life of desire, then left the family. They first practiced ascetic life, later converted to middle path, and finally realized the unsurpassed, perfect, and universal enlightenment. This is how the Thus-Comers demonstrate the transformed body in an expedient and skillful way."

Manjusri Bodhisattva asked the Buddha again, "World-Honored One, how many different kinds of words and voices were used by the transformed bodies of the Thus-Comers to teach the sentient beings, so the immature would become mature, and the mature would become liberated quickly?"

The Buddha replied to Manjusri Bodhisattva, "Good gentleman, three kinds of words and voices were used in the Thus-Comers' teachings: sutra (texts), vinaya (precepts), and matrka (treatises)."

"World-Honored One, what is the sutra? What is the vinaya? And what is the matrka?"

"Manjusri, the sutra means 'I will use the things I have absorbed here and now to reveal various dharmas.' These things are divided into four categories, nine categories, or twenty-nine categories.

"What are the four categories of the things contained in the sutras? They are the things about hearing correct teachings, the things to which the practitioners will aspire, the things about cultivation and learning, and the things about the bodhi.

"What are the nine categories of the things? They are: (1) The things about the establishment of the sentient beings.[2] (2) The things received by the sentient beings.[3] (3) The things about the twelve chains of dependent origination. (4) The things about the four kinds of food for nurturing the sentient beings. (5) The things about contamination and purification.[4] (6) The things about the differences of numberless dharma realms. (7) The things about the ones who can teach; namely, the Buddhas and their disciples. (8) The things about what are taught.[5] (9) The things about the assemblies and the audiences.

"What are the twenty-nine categories of the things? As to the contaminated dharmas, there are four categories. (1) All

---

2   This means that the Thus-Comers have used the teaching of the five aggregates, namely, matter, feeling, thinking, action, and consciousness, to establish the sentient beings.

3   This indicates the six inner spheres that receive the stimuli from the six outer spheres so as to form the twelve spheres.

4   This means the four noble truths.

5   This means the factors for enlightenment.

phenomena of the conditioned dharmas. (2) The conditioned dharmas that are drifting in sequence. (3) The attachment to the selfness of individuals as the cause of reincarnation in the lives to come. (4) The attachment to the self-nature of dharmas that also serves as the causes of reincarnation in the lives to come.

"As to the pure dharmas, there are twenty-five categories. (1) Staying in the correct mindfulness of the correct dharma after hearing it. (2) Reflecting on the correct dharma diligently. (3) Letting the mind dwell peacefully in meditation. (4) Letting the mind dwell joyfully in meditation and enjoy the worldly dharmas appearing presently. (5) The expedient way of contemplating the four noble truths to transcend the flawed causes and conditions of suffering in the three realms. (6) Knowing comprehensively the noble truth of suffering. This again contains three kinds of knowledge: comprehensive knowledge about the causes of the upside-down thinking in the realm of desire, the comprehensive knowledge about incorrect thoughts and actions in the realm of form, and the comprehensive knowledge about arrogance in the realm of formless. (7) Undertaking cultivation in order to terminate the causes of suffering. (8) Working toward nirvana in order to cease suffering. (9) Practicing the path for the cessation of suffering. (10) After reaching the phase of seeing the path, the practitioners will not regress in cultivation. (11) The things about mental images. (12) The things about the sixteen kinds of mental images perceived when contemplating the four noble truths in the realm of desire and the upper realm.[6] (13) The things about skillful contemplation of the vex-

---

6　When contemplating the four noble truths of the realm of desire and the upper realm (the realm of form and the realm of formlessness) in order to elicit flawless knowledge, there are eight kinds of mental images for each realm; therefore there are sixteen kinds of mental images in total.

ations terminated and the vexations not yet terminated. (14) The things about restless and chaotic minds. (15) The concentrations that make our minds not restless and chaotic. (16) The basis upon which the not restless minds rely. (17) The things about diligent cultivation with additional efforts. (18) The superior benefits derived from cultivation and learning. (19) The solid, nonregressive effects of cultivation. (20) The things about the holy ones' great actions. (21) Blessings and wisdom caused by holy actions. (22) Thorough and insightful understanding of the reality. (23) The things about the realization of nirvana. (24) The correct views of the world derived from learning vinaya well taught by the Buddha to transcend all views of other-path practitioners. (25) The things about regression when staying away from cultivation. Regression means discontinuation of the cultivation of vinaya. Those who make mistakes in cultivation are not named regression.

"Manjusri, vinaya means the methods of individual liberation and correspondent dharmas that I have demonstrated and explained for the voice-hearers and bodhisattvas."

"World-Honored One, what is the content of individual liberation teaching for the bodhisattvas?"

"Good gentleman, you must know that there are seven main fields in this regard. The first is the teaching of the rules and rituals that bodhisattvas should observe. The second is the teaching about the superior laws[7] that bodhisattvas should follow so that they will become superior. The third is the teaching about the violation of the precepts. The fourth is the teaching

---

7   There are four superior laws for bodhisattvas to become superior: do not boast yourself and dispise others; do not be stingy and reluctant in practicing giving; do not get angry and hate; and do not slander the texts of bodhisattva path. Please refer to Venerable Yen Pei, *Jei Shen Mi Jing Yu Ti Shi*, Taipei: Heavenly Lotus Publishing, 1988, pp. 590-591.

about the practitioners who incline to violate precepts. The fifth is the teaching about the practitioners who do not violate precepts. The sixth is the teaching about repentance. The seventh is the teaching about discarding the rules and rituals."

"Manjusri, the matrka has eleven forms that I use to reveal and expound the natures and characteristics of various dharmas. What are these eleven forms? The first is the form of the world. The second is the form of the ultimate meaning. The third is the form of the factors for enlightenment. The fourth is the form of the transient beings. The fifth is the form of self-nature. The sixth is the form of the effects. The seventh is the form of receiving the teachings. The eighth is the form of hindering the pursuit of the dharma. The ninth is the form of following and being compliant with the dharma. The tenth is the form of faults and mistakes. The eleventh is the form of superior benefits.

"The form of the world that the Buddha teaches consists of three kinds. The first is the teaching about the individuals in reincarnation. The second is the teaching about the self-natures of universal attachment. The third is the teaching about the karmic causes and effects of all dharmas in their operations.

"The form of the ultimate meaning comprises the teaching of the seven kinds of realness.

"The form of the factors for enlightenment is the teaching about all kinds of things that should be known comprehensively.

"The form of the transient beings means the teaching about the contemplations of the phenomena of all dharmas in eight areas.

"What are the contemplations of the phenomena of all dharmas in eight areas? The first is the contemplation of the reality.

The second is the contemplation of establishments. The third is the contemplation of the faults. The fourth is the contemplation of the merits and virtues. The fifth is the contemplation of the essential meanings. The sixth is the contemplation of drifting. The seventh is the contemplation of the principles. The eighth is the contemplation through general and particular perspectives.

"The contemplation of reality means contemplating the realness of all dharmas. The contemplation of establishments means contemplating the establishment of the individuals in reincarnation; the establishment of the natures of universal attachment; the establishment of the ways of teaching either by giving direct and explicit lectures, by elucidating meanings respectively, by asking questions instead of answering questions, and by keeping silent; and the establishment of conferring prophecies implicitly or explicitly of the achievement that the learners will fulfill in the future. The contemplation of the faults means contemplating varied faults caused by numberless contaminated gates as I have lectured on. The contemplation of the merits and virtues means contemplating varied superior benefits caused by numberless pure gates as I have taught.

"There are six kinds of essential meanings: the meaning of the reality; the meaning of the realization of the truth; the meaning of the teaching and guidance; the meaning of staying far away from two extremes; the meaning of the inconceivable; and the meaning of speaking either by following lecturer's interest or by following audience's interest.

"The contemplation of drifting means contemplating the

three forms of the conditioned dharmas[8] in the three phases of time[9] under the four kinds of conditions.[10]

"The contemplation of the principles means contemplating the principle of dependent origination, the principle of operations, the principle of realization and attainment, and the principle of the dharma as it has always been.

"The principle of dependent origination means that the causes and conditions will give rise to various dharmas, and the relevant concepts and languages are created accordingly. The principle of operations means that after the dharmas arise owning to the combination of causes and conditions, they will accomplish various operations and thus bring about more karmas. The principle of realization and attainment means that the causes and conditions will also make these things—the statements, the evidences or reasons to support the statements, and the examples used to prove them—possible, so the learners are able to realize the bodhi and attain enlightenment.

"Briefly speaking, there are also two kinds of principles: the pure ones and the impure ones. The dharmas are pure because of five conditions and they are impure because of other seven conditions. The five pure principles are: The knowledge is formed through direct perception. The knowledge is not formed through direct perception but based on the perceived knowledge. The knowledge is formed by analogy. The knowledge is formed by perfect realization. And the teaching is given with virtuous and pure words.

---

8   The three forms of conditioned dharmas are the form of arising, the form of duration, and the form of extinction.

9   The three phases of time are the past, present, and future.

10   The four kinds of conditions are cause and condition, consecutive thoughts in sequence, the conditions that stimulate the mind, and the conditions that reinforce main causes.

"The knowledge formed through direct perception means that we experience and observe that all phenomena are impermanent and with suffering, and all dharmas are without self-natures. We come to this conclusion through direct observation of the world. This is named the directly perceived knowledge.

"The knowledge formed based on perceived knowledge means that we can get to know something indirectly but based on the directly perceived knowledge, such as all phenomena are transient; all phenomena change instantaneously; the natures of the pure and impure karmas in the past remain indestructible. Based on the visible changing phenomena we generalize that all dharmas are impermanent. Based on the different results caused by various karmas we generalize that different karmas bring about different effects. We also generalize that pure karmas bring about desirable effects while impure karmas undesirable effects. Although we do not perceive the objects directly, we can get to know them indirectly through comparison and generalization. This is named the knowledge based on the perceived knowledge.

"The knowledge formed by analogy means that in inner and outer aggregates of dharmas, we may attain analogous knowledge from the common experiences and the realization shared by all. For instance, we may get to know that birth and death are universal in the world; the suffering of birth, old age, and so forth of the world are universal in the world; uneasiness of living in the world is universal; and the fact that one's prosperity and decay will come and go is also universal in the world. This is named the knowledge formed by analogy.

"The knowledge formed through perfect realization means

that perfect realization definitely can be achieved by means of the knowledge directly perceived, based on perceived knowledge, and by analogy.

"The teaching given with virtuous and pure words indicates the teachings given by the wise ones. They are the teachings, for instance, on nirvana, ultimate tranquility, and so forth. Good gentleman, these five pure principles show us the pure paths for contemplating the truths. Because they are pure, they are worthy of cultivation and learning."

Manjusri Bodhisattva asked the Buddha again, "World-Honored One, what are the features of the wise ones?"

The Buddha replied to Manjusri Bodhisattva, "Good gentleman, there are five features of the wise ones. As the wise ones appear in the world, their voices will be universally heard. They all have thirty-two perfect major marks. They fully possess the ten abilities and are able to cease the doubts and puzzles of all sentient beings. They fully possess the four kinds of fearlessness and are able to teach correct dharma widely; they will not be subjugated by other-path arguments but can subjugate and destroy all incorrect arguments. In their well-taught vinaya, the noble eight path and the four sramana effects are accessible and attainable. There are five features of the wise ones: their birth in the world, their perfect marks, their abilities to terminate the nets of puzzles of all sentient beings, their abilities to subjugate other-path arguments, and the benefits they will bring to the holy-path practitioners and monastics.

"Good gentleman, the realization and attainment of the perfect truth is thus made possible by direct perception, by reasoning, or by the teachings given by the holy ones. The five principles mentioned above are named the pure principles.

"What are the seven impure principles? The first is to think that this dharma and other dharmas in the same category should share common characteristics. The second is to think that this dharma and other dharmas in different categories should have different characteristics. The third is to think that all dharmas in the same category should share the same characteristics. The fourth is to think that the dharmas in different categories should have different characteristics. The fifth is to make generalizations incorrectly from different categories. The sixth is the incorrect reasoning that does not lead to perfect realization. The seventh is the not virtuous and impure teachings.

"As the dharmas share same characteristics, they can be grouped in the same category. As individual dharmas have their own particular characteristics, natures, karmas, and causes and effects and thus appear as distinct from other dharmas, they will be grouped in different categories. Good gentleman, if we adopt the dharmas in the same category but with different characteristics to make an analogy, or if we adopt an example from different category to make an analogy, then the conclusion thereupon will not be definite, so it is not a perfect realization. If the dharmas in different categories happen to have certain common characteristics, then our conclusion based on such an analogy will not be definite, so it is not a perfect realization either. Because of imperfect realization, the contemplation and investigation of the truth will not be pure. Because they are not pure, they should not be learned and practiced. Both the generalizations made from different categories and the not virtuous and impure teachings are not good either in their forms or their natures.

"The principle of the dharma as it has always been means

that whether the Thus-Comers appear in the world or not, the dharma nature dwells peacefully in dharma dwelling and in dharma realm at all times.

"The principle of contemplating the phenomena of all beings from both general and particular perspectives means that general description will be given first, while particular elaborations will be demonstrated later.

"The fifth form of matrka is the form of self-nature. It means the factors for enlightenment that the learners should adopt and rely on, such as the four bases of correct mindfulness, four correct endeavors, and so forth. The sixth form of attaining effects means that the merits and virtues as the effects of and beyond the world are caused by the termination of all vexations. The seventh form of receiving teachings means that after receiving the teachings for liberation, the bodhisattvas should lecture on and explain extensively what they have received for others. The eighth form of hindering the pursuit of the dharma indicates the obstacles the practitioners may encounter when cultivating the factors for the bodhi. The ninth form of being compliant with the dharma means that the practitioners should cultivate diligently by following the correct dharma. The tenth form of faults and mistakes means all faults and mistakes caused by the obstacles. The eleventh form of superior benefits means all merits and virtues resulting from following the correct paths."

Manjusri Bodhisattva said to the Buddha, "We do hope the World-Honored One will briefly teach us the dharani meaning of sutra, vinaya, and matrka not shared by other paths so the bodhisattvas are able to insightfully understand the profound secret meaning of various dharmas that the Thus-Comer teaches."

The Buddha replied to Manjusri Bodhisattva, "Good gentleman, now listen to me carefully! I am going to tell you the dharani meaning not shared by other paths so that the bodhisattvas can well understand the secret meaning implied by my words.

"As I say, good gentleman, all pure and impure dharmas do not have operations. There are no individuals in reincarnation either. It is because all kinds of dharmas are without doing. It is not that all dharmas are impure inherently and then become pure; nor are they pure inherently, contaminated in later times, and then purified. Because of the heavy vexations, the ordinary sentient beings are attached to the thinking that the dharmas and individuals have different self-natures. Owing to the hidden roots of vexations and incorrect views, they misunderstand that the 'I' and the associated images are existent. Because of this delusion, they insist that I see, I hear, I smell, I taste, I touch, I know, I eat, I do, I am contaminated, I am purified, and so forth. As this kind of thinking continues, more and more incorrect views will be generated. If we can understand all dharmas as they really are, all heavy bondages will be terminated permanently. Then we will have no more vexations, stay far away from all nonsensical arguments, and become extremely pure. We will rely on nothing and do not have additional effort. Briefly speaking, good gentleman, this is the dharani meaning not shared by other paths."

At that time, the World-Honored One reiterated this meaning in verse:

All contaminated and pure dharmas are without operations,

There are no so-called individuals in reincarnation.
I have said that all dharmas do not have doing,
No earlier or later appear the contaminated or the pure
*   dharmas.*

Owing to heavy vexations, hidden roots, and incorrect views
Sentient beings are attached to the "I" and the associated
*   images.*
Based on the delusion of selfness and so forth, they believe
*   that*
I eat, I do, I am contaminated, and I am purified.

If we can understand all dharmas as they really are,
All heavy vexations will be terminated permanently.
We'll be free from contamination, purification, and nonsensi-
*   cal arguments,*
And will rely on nothing and have no more additional effort.

At that time, Manjusri Great Bodhisattva asked the Buddha again, "World-Honored One, how do we know the arising of the Thus-Comer's minds?"

The Buddha replied to Manjusri Bodhisattva, "Good gentleman, the Thus-Comer is not manifested by the arising of mind consciousness; rather, it arises so spontaneously and effortlessly just like a transformation."

Manjusri Bodhisattva asked the Buddha again, "World-Honored One, if the dharma body of various Thus-Comers is far away from all deliberate efforts, how can their minds arise?"

The Buddha replied to Manjusri Bodhisattva, "Good gentleman, it is because of the power of the additional deliberate efforts made previously in cultivating and learning expedient prajna that let their minds arise. Good gentleman, someone fell asleep unconsciously and then tried to wake up. It was not the deliberate effort made right at the moment when he was trying to wake up but because of the effort made previously that made him awake. Someone entered the concentration of the extinction of thinking and feeling and then tried to rise. It was not because of the effort deliberately made at the moment when he was trying to rise from the concentration, but because of the influence of the effort made previously that made him rise from concentration. So are the Thus-Comers' minds. It is because of the influence of the efforts made previously that make their minds arise."

Manjusri Bodhisattva asked the Buddha again, "World-Honored One, does the transformed body of the Thus-Comer have mind? Does he have no mind?"

The Buddha replied to Manjusri Bodhisattva, "Good gentleman, we may say that he has mind; we may also say that he has no mind. Why? The Thus-Comer does not have intention to have his mind arise, but he indeed may do it spontaneously to satisfy sentient beings' wishes."

Manjusri Bodhisattva asked the Buddha again, "World-Honored One, what is the difference between the areas in which the Thus-Comers act and dwell, and the realms in which the Thus-Comers offer services?"

The Buddha replied to Manjusri Bodhisattva, "Good gentleman, the areas in which the Thus-Comers act and dwell are various inconceivable pure Buddha lands shared by all Thus-Comers. These Buddha lands have numberless merits and virtues and are dignified by all wonderful things. There are five realms in which the Buddhas offer services. They are the realm of the sentient beings, the realm of the physical world, the dharma realm, the realm of the tamed ones, and the realm of taming others expediently. This is the difference between these two things."

Manjusri Bodhisattva again asked the Buddha, "World-Honored One, when the Thus-Comers realize and attain the perfect and universal enlightenment, turn the correct dharma wheel, and then enter great nirvana, what are the forms of these three phases?"

The Buddha replied to Manjusri Bodhisattva, "Good gentleman, you must know that all these three periods do not have dualistic forms: The Thus-Comers have neither attained nor not attained the perfect and universal enlightenment; they have neither turned nor not turned the correct dharma wheel; they have neither entered nor not entered great nirvana. Why? It is because the dharma body of the Thus-Comers is pure in the final analysis, and the transformed body of the Thus-Comers has manifested and demonstrated itself at all times."

Manjusri Bodhisattva asked the Buddha again, "World-Honored One, the sentient beings will obtain a lot of merits and virtues only if they can see, hear, serve, and make offerings to the transformed body of the Thus-Comer. What is the relationship between Thus-Comer and sentient beings?"

The Buddha replied to Manjusri Bodhisattva, "Good gentleman, the Thus-Comer can increase the powers of the existing positive causes and conditions already held by the sentient beings, while the transformed body is the locus where the Thus-Comers' powers reside."

Manjusri Bodhisattva asked the Buddha again, "World-

Honored One, although the dharma body of the Thus-Comer has no additional efforts, it can emit great light of wisdom and demonstrate innumerable images of the transformed body for various sentient beings. How does it do this? Why the liberation body of the voice-hearers and self-enlightened ones cannot do so?"

The Buddha replied to Manjusri Bodhisattva, "Good gentleman, the fire crystal and water crystal can emit brilliant lights effortlessly by reflecting the lights of the sun and moon, but they cannot do this without sun and moon. So with the support of great power, authority, merits, and virtues of the Thus-Comer, the sentient beings can increase their powers of positive karmas. The skillful craftsman is capable of carving words and figures well on the surface of pearls; without skillful craftsman's work the pearls cannot shine with beautiful words and figures by themselves. It is through the cultivation and learning of the expedient prajna in innumerable dharma realms that the dharma body of the Thus-Comer has been sharpened and moulded and become perfect. That is why the dharma body can emit great and brilliant light of wisdom and manifest various images of transformed body, while the liberation body cannot."

Manjusri Bodhisattva asked the Buddha again, "World-Honored One, as you say, both Thus-Comers and bodhisattvas possess great powers, authority, and virtues, so with their support and protection the sentient beings can be reborn in the noble family of Ksatriya or the noble family of Brahman in the realm of desire and have perfect human bodies and great wealth; or can be reborn in the heavens in the realm of desire, the realm of form, and the realm of formlessness and all have perfect body and wealth. World-Honored One, what are the secret meanings implied by this?"

The Buddha replied to Manjusri Bodhisattva, "Good gentleman, the Thus-Comers and bodhisattvas always propagate the correct path and its cultivation and teach the sentient beings according to their individual needs with great powers, authority, and virtues so the sentient beings can obtain perfect bodies and great wealth. If the sentient beings follow the teachings to cultivate and practice the correct path and correct actions, they will certainly attain perfect bodies and great wealth. If they act contrary to this correct path, look down on the teachings and slander them with contempt, annoyance, and hatred, they will be reborn in bad destinies and will live in poverty with inferior bodies. Manjusri, because of this cause and condition, the great powers and virtues of the Thus-Comers and bodhisattvas can bring sentient beings perfect body and wealth, but it does not mean that they can ensure that the negative–karma makers will not fall in bad destinies and be reborn in poverty with inferior bodies."

Manjusri Bodhisattva asked the Buddha again, "World-Honored One, in filthy lands what things happen often and what things happen seldom?"

The Buddha replied to Manjusri Bodhisattva, "Good gentleman, in filthy lands eight things are frequent while two things are rare. What are the eight things that happen often? The first is the other-path practice. The second is the sentient beings in suffering. The third is the wide gap between different castes. The fourth is a lot of negative conducts. The fifth is the violation of laws and the lack of respect toward precepts. The sixth is the rebirth in inferior destinies. The seventh is the pursuit of the inferior vehicle. The eighth is the weak intention for practicing bodhisattva path. Two things happen seldom: The bodhisattvas gather together to joyfully pursue the bodhi and the Thus-Comer appears in the world. But in the pure lands, on the contrary, the first eight things happen rarely while the latter two things happen often."

At that time, Manjusri Great Bodhisattva asked the Buddha, "World-Honored One, what is the name of this dharma gate for explaining the profound secret? How should we practice it?"

The Buddha replied to Manjusri Great Bodhisattva, "Good gentleman, this is named the ultimate meaning of the things fulfilled by the Thus-Comer. All of you should accept, embrace, and practice it."

When the Buddha was teaching the ultimate meaning of the things fulfilled by the Thus-Comer, seventy-five thousand great bodhisattvas in the assembly realized and attained the perfect dharma body.

Translator's Introduction

Why this sutra is unique

The Sutra of Explaining the Profound Secret, translated by Master Xuanzang from the Sanskrit *Samdhinirmocana Sutra*, is a record of the Buddha's teachings on mind consciousness, the theory of knowledge, the reality of existent beings, and the yoga path of samatha and vipasyana practice in the ten stages of bodhisattva cultivation. The secret meanings implied in sutra, vinaya, and matrka, the three areas of Sakyamuni Buddha's teachings, as well as all inconceivable exquisite things accomplished by the Thus-Comer are also well explicated.

This sutra provides bases for building Buddhist philosophy of mind and knowledge, ontology, and the learning contents and methods of bodhisattva education. It has nurtured the development of Yogacara Buddhism in India and its expansion in eastern Asia. It has made one of the two main streams of great-vehicle Buddhism unfold, extend, spread, and shine brilliantly. *Samdhinirmocana Sutra* has contributed together with *Yogacara Bhumi Sastra* and other treatises written by Asanga and Vasubandhu to the formation of Yogacara school. This is the only one extant sutra in this tradition, while all other writings of this lineage available today are only in the form of treatise.

The name "sutra" is given to the teachings directly said by the Buddha but were recorded posthumously. The Buddha's teachings first appeared in a text form in the first Buddhist canonical council of 500 arhats convened by leading monk Mahakasyapa in Rajagrha (Rajgir) after Buddha entered nirvana. In this council the Buddha's words were recited by Anada, then the senior monastics in the council examined what he recited. They discussed, came to agreement or disagreement, or just made some changes. The vinaya (precepts for the monastics) set up by their teacher the Buddha were also recited by Upali in this council.

Ananda had been Buddha's attendant for a long time and was privileged to hear what the Buddha said most of the time. More importantly he had inconceivable memory of what he heard. In the history of Buddhism in India we may see some other important councils held for compiling scriptures. The Buddha's teachings were usually transmitted through dharani, an art of retention after hearing and learning; an efficient way of memorizing Buddha's words and his dialogues with others before his words were transformed into texts. The style of sutra is different from matrka or sastra. The sastra entertains a relatively well-organized structure with discursive logical reasoning, most of which were written by Buddhist scholars beginning around 300 BCE, the so-called secretarian age when the sangha community began to split into more than a dozen sects.

We may trace the original thoughts of Yogacara and other Buddhist denominations back to *Agama*, a rich, fresh wellspring in which the sources of inspiring ideas have nurtured different vehicles of Buddhism practitioners, featuring with the hearing, reflection, and cultivation of the four noble truths along with the theory of dependent origination as main topics.

In *Samyukt-agama* the Buddha said that the laws of the world are already there as they have always been, not invented by him or others. He said that he discovered the universe rules just like his great immortal holy ancestors did. And as his ancestors, he followed up to unveil them to the sentient beings. As human and other sentient beings suffer in reincarnation endlessly mainly because of the lack of correct knowledge of the phenomena of the world and the rules of the world, the fully enlightened ones are obliged to elaborate, demonstrate, and explain expediently and skillfully the truth of the world, the so-called dharma, for all sentient beings so as to let them hear the correct dharma, walk on the right path, and benefit greatly. Therefore the Buddha at all times teaches the four groups of followers why the individuals reincarnate in birth and death and suffer and how they should learn and cultivate to become liberated. He also teaches the names and concepts of the aggregates, spheres, realms, and so forth and the laws of the arising and extinction of all existent beings in the world. He tries all possible ways to let them realize that the arising of all existent beings and relevant phenomena are caused by the combination of causes and conditions. Where there is arising, there is extinction. As arising means a combination of causes and conditions, extinction means their disintegration. Causes and conditions are always in change, so the characteristics of every transient existence of the dharmas are impermanent. It is also real that not a single cause or condition can alone make the dependent origination happen.[11]

This *Samdhinirmocana Sutra* is not lengthy; rather, it is a rel-

---

11 *Samyuktagama*, Fascicle 12, verses 287 and 299, in Chinese, translated by Gunabhadra (394-468 CE).

atively short, dialectic, yet succinct canon in which many basic crucial ideas of Buddhist epistemology and mind philosophy originate. Although it records the words of the Buddha's dialogues with several highly enlightened bodhisattvas, its writing style is quite similar to sastra (treatise) as the dialogues wherein unfold in a discursive and logically reasoning process—a writing style shared by most of sastras but rare in sutras.

The basic concepts of mind consciousness and the theory of knowledge are demonstrated through the detailed, concrete, and step-by-step delineation of the bodhisattva-path practice so the practitioners are able to follow and benefit in their cultivation toward perfect enlightenment. It is reasonable to say that the natures and implied meanings of knowledge and mind consciousness taught by the Buddha in this sutra are established for paving the way for bodhisattvas' learning and cultivation, leading to the perfect enlightenment and liberation of the world and beyond the world.

Therefore, this sutra is unique not only because it is the only extant sutra that serves as the origin of Yagacara Buddhism or it is presented in matrka style, but also because it provides the solid foundation for bodhisattva-path education. The Buddha himself was an educator, philosopher, and psychologist even in terms of modern scholarly classification. His comprehensive contemplation and in-depth understanding of human cognition, as well as his insightful description of the formation of knowledge and wisdom, may inspire the epistemologists and mind philosophers of our time.

The entire text of this Xuanzang's translation was quoted except the first chapter in *Treatise on the Stages of Yoga Prac-*

tice (*Yogacara-bhumi Sastra*), authored by Asanga, or allegedly taught or dictated by Maitreya Bodhisattva. In *The Treatise on the Establishment of the Consciousness-Only Doctrine* (*Cheng-wei-shi lun*),[12] six sutras[13] and eleven treatises[14] were often quoted or cited. But among these origins of consciousness-only philosophy, the basic sutra is *The Sutra of Explaining the Profound Secret,* and the basic treatise is the *Yogacara-bhumi Sastra.*[15]

---

12   *The Treatise on the Establishment of the Consciousness-Only Doctrine*, compiled and translated by Xuanzang is mainly based on Dharmapala's (530-561 CE) interpretation of Vasubandhu's *Thirty Verses of Consciousness-Only*, but into which other nine Yogacara scholars' interpretations were also merged. This treatise became very influential since the seventh century in China and other areas in Asia.

13   The six sutras are (1) *Avatamsaka Sutra* (*Hua Yen Jing*), translated into Chinese by Buddhabhadra around 420 CE in 60 fascicles and Siksananda around 699 CE in 80 fascicles. (2) *Samdhinirmocana Sutra* (*The Sutra of Explaining the Profound Secret; Jie Shen Mi Jing*), translated by Xuanzang in 647; other Chinese translations were also made by Bodhiruci in 514 CE, Paramita in 557 CE, and Gunabhadra in 435-43 CE. (3) *Lankavatara sutra*, there are three Chinese versions by Guṇabhadra, Bodhiruci, and Śikṣānanda. (4) *The Sutra of the Dignified Merits of Tathagata's Appearance, Abhidharma Sutra*, and *Hou Yen Sutra* were mentioned, but they were not translated into Chinese and their original texts were not available.

14   The eleven treatises are (1) *Yogacarabhumi Sastra* (*Stages of Yoga Practice Treatise; Yu Chieh Shih Ti Lun*), 100 fascicles, by Maitreya, translated into Chinese by Xuanzang in 648 CE. (2) *Aryavacaprakarana Sastra* (*Hsien Yang Sheng Chiao Lun*), 20 fascicles, by Asanga, translated by Xuanzang in 645 CE. (3) *Mahāyāna Sūtrālamkāra Kārikā*, by Asanga, in 13 fascicles (24 chapters), translated into Chinese by Prabhakaramitra (565-633 CE).(4) *Pramana-samuccaya* (*Compendium of the Rules of Logic*) by Dignaga, two Chinese versions, translated by Paramartha and Yi-jing. (5) *Mahayanasamgraha; She Ta Sheng lun* (Encyclopedia of Mahayana), 3 fascicles, by Asanga, translated by Xuanzang in 649 CE. (6) *Treatise of Ten Stages Sutra* by Vasubandhu, translated into Chinese by Bodhiruci, 12 fascicles. (7) *The Treatise of Ultimate Meaning of Yoga* (*Feng Bie Yoga Lun*), lectured by Maitreya; the original treatise is missing and not translated into Chinese, but was mentioned and quoted by Asanga in his *Mahayana-samgraha*. Master Ying Shun said that this treatise was relevant to Chapter 6 of *Samdhinir-mocana*, "The Ultimate Meaning of Yoga," focusing mainly on samatha and vypasyana. (8) *Alambanapariksa* (*Treatise of Contemplating Objective Conditions; Kuan So Yuan Yuan Lun*), 1 fascle, by Dignaga, translated by Xuanzang in 657 CE. (9) *Vimsatika-vrtti* (Twenty Verses on Vijnapti-matra Treatise; *Wei Shih Erh Shih Lun*), by Vasubandhu, translated by Xuanzang in 661 CE. (10) *Pien chung pien lun* (*Madhyantavibhaga bhasya; Treatise on Distinguishing between Middle and Extremes, Bien Chung Bien Lun*), by Vasubandhu, translated by Xuanzang in 661 CE. (11) *Abhidharmasamuccaya-vyakhya* (*Mahayana Abhidharma Mixed-Collection Treatise, Ta Sheng A Pi Ta Mo*), 16 fascicles, Sthiramati's commentary to Asanga's *Abhidharma-samuccaya*, translated by Xuanzang in 646 CE.

15   Please refer to *A Commentary on Chengweishilun* (*A Commentary of the Treatise on the Establishment of Consciousness-Only Doctrine*), Kueiji, fascicle 1, in *Taisho Tripitaka*, Vol. 43, No. 1830.

Different versions of translation of this sutra

There are at least two English translations in print today in addition to the present one. One is John Powers' *Wisdom of Buddha*, published by Dharma Publishing, rendered in 1995 from a Tibetan text. The other one is John P. Keenan's *The Scripture on the Explication of Underlying Meaning*, published by Numata Center for Buddhist Translation and Research in 2000. I would like to express my appreciation for their efforts in propagating Buddhism.

The present, unabridged translation of the Chinese version rendered by Master Xuanzang from Sanskrit contains eight chapters distributed in five fascicles. The first, second, and the third chapters are contained in the first fascicle; the fourth and fifth chapters are contained in the second fascicle; from the third through the fifth fascicle there is only one chapter in each fascicle.

The original Sanskrit *Samdhinirmocana Sutra* is not available today. It was first rendered into Chinese with the title *Xiang Xu Jie Tuo Jing* (*Sutra of Consecutive Liberation*) in the fourth century by Gunabhadra (394-478), a Buddhist monk from central India who went to China in 435. This partially translated edition comprises only two chapters; one should be equivalent to the seventh chapter, and the other the eighth chapter, of the Xuanzang's version.

But Xuanzang was not the first one making the whole text in Chinese. Over one hundred years before him a monk from northern India named Bodhiruci arrived at Loyang, then the capital of China, in 508 during the Dynasty of North Wei. He was very active for translating Buddhist sutras into Chinese, and one of his works was *Sheng Mi Jei Tuo Jing* (*The Sutra of the Profound and Secret Liberation*), the first complete Chinese *Samdhinirmocana Sutra* which contains eleven chapters distributed in five fascicles.

Later in the sixth century, Paramartha (499-569) went to China from northwestern India and translated one chapter of the sutra into Chinese between 557 and 569, which is equivalent to the second chapter of Xuanzang's version.

Xuanzang (602?-664) was born in China in the sovereignty of Sui, a very short dynasty lasting only for 37 years. He left China in 628 in the second decade of the founding of Tang dynasty. After a very difficult journey he finally arrived in India, where he went to Nalanda University and learned yagacara sutra and relevant treatises from **Śīlabhadra**, the leading monastic scholar and one of the most important Buddhist logicians of all time, who was already over 100 years old at that time. Xuanzang also made a lot of travels around India to visit with Buddhist scholars, having in-depth conversations with them, and sought Sanskrit sutras and treatises for bringing them back to China in order to translate them into Chinese. He became the university instructor and was very well known in India, widely respected owing to his erudition, talent of debate, and the insightful understanding of Buddhist texts. He came back to China in 645, carrying 657 different titles of Sanskrit Buddhist texts contained in 520 boxes. His translation career lasted for nineteen years, and 75 titles in 1335 fascicles of Chinese translation were produced by him. He has influenced enormously and extensively the development of Buddhism.

Both Bodhiruci and Xuanzang translations have five fascicles. Bodhiruci divided the first fascicle into six chapters while Xuanzang made it three chapters. Therefore, Bodhiruci's translation consists of 11 chapters while Xuanzang's has 8 chapters.

Summary of the main thoughts in this sutra

The eight chapters are

1. Preface: The causes and conditions of the assembly

2. The forms of the ultimate meaning

3. The forms of the mind consciousness

4. The forms of all dharmas

5. The phenomena of selflessness

6. The ultimate meaning of yoga

7. The ultimate meaning of the stages of paramita

8. The things fulfilled by the Thus-Comer

Chapter 1
Preface: The causes and conditions of the assembly

In this chapter the magnificent merits and virtues of the Thus-Comer and his inconceivable spiritual level were described. The Buddha emitted lights to illumine the worlds that were without boundary and temporality. His virtues and merits were so superb, glorious, and dignified. His mindfulness and wisdom were perfect. His consciousness was wonderfully pure. His samatha and vypasyana were the uppermost. He had always dwelled in extreme self-ease and freedom. He had also attained the liberation gates of emptiness, formlessness, and nonaspiration. The Buddha demonstrated the superior effects that he had achieved in order to inspire and encourage the sentient beings to pursue the Buddha path. His virtuous roots would arise with extreme self-ease. His consciousness was always with pure form. He embraced the widely expanding delight of dharma taste and was dedicated to bringing justice and benefits to all sentient beings so that their vexations, disasters, and defilements would be removed. They would be able to get rid of evil demons. This is exactly the path that the great bodhisattvas are looking for.

Wherever the Thus-Comer stayed, he would be surrounded and followed by great voice-hearers, great bodhisattvas, and numberless heavenly and human beings.

The great voice-hearers present in the assembly were all well released in wisdom and well liberated in mind. They observed pure precepts, practiced the holy teachings given by the Buddha, and enjoyed the dharma. They heard and learned much and retained well. They had gained present dharma joy and dwelled in great pure field of bliss. They behaved in dignified and tranquil demeanors; they act and spoke with great patience.

The great bodhisattvas coming to this assembly from different Buddha lands had all stayed in the great vehicle, treated all sentient beings equally, stayed away from differentiation and nondifferentiation, subjugated all devils, and cared about all sentient beings. The leading great bodhisattvas present in the assembly were Understanding Profound Secret Meaning Great Bodhisattva, Asking Reasonably Great Bodhisattva, Dharma Flowing Great Bodhisattva, Virtuous Pure Wisdom Great Bodhisattva, Broad Wisdom Great Bodhisattva, Virtue Base

Great Bodhisattva, Ultimate Meaning Arising Great Bodhisattva, Contemplating-in-Freedom Great Bodhisattva, Maitreya Great Bodhisattva, and Manjusri Great Bodhisattva.

Chapter 2
The forms of the ultimate meaning

In the beginning of the second chapter, the conversations between Understanding Profound Secret Meaning Great Bodhisattva and Asking Reasonably Great Bodhisattva had focused on the topic of the two kinds of dharmas: the conditioned dharmas that are caused by dependent origination, restricted by causes and conditions, and are constantly in change; and the unconditioned dharmas that are always as they have been and are without condition and change. When replying to Asking Reasonably Bodhisattva who raised the questions of what the designated name of "all dharmas" means and why all dharmas are without duality, Understanding Profound Secret Meaning Bodhisattva said that there are two kinds of dharmas: the conditioned and the unconditioned. But he added that the conditioned dharmas are neither conditioned nor unconditioned, and the unconditioned dharmas are neither unconditioned nor conditioned; therefore, they are not dualistic. Why? It is because this dichotomy is created by the Buddha as an expediency for teaching ordinary sentient beings in order to let them get rid of the attachment to names and languages and realize what the phenomena of the world really are. Understanding Profound Secret Meaning Bodhisattva demonstrated with similes that both the conditioned and the unconditioned dharmas are just the terms established provisionally and unreal. The holy ones attain universal enlightenment because they are free from the attachment to languages. The ordinary sentient beings cannot realize that the reality of the world is apart from names and words, so they are unable to attain real liberation and self-ease and suffer in endless birth and death. The establishment of the conditioned dharma as opposed to the unconditioned dharma is a skillful way to guide them to self-enlightenment. When asserting that the conditioned dharmas are neither conditioned nor unconditioned, and the unconditioned dharmas are neither unconditioned nor conditioned, what is really meant is that not only the conditioned dharmas, but also the unconditioned, dharmas are unreal; they are thus nondualistic in essence.

In the second part of the second chapter, Dharma Flowing Great Bodhisattva acclaimed that the Thus-Comer's birth is very unusual. Because of his appearance in the world, the sentient beings are privileged to access the ultimate truth. The Buddha commended that the ultimate meanings he teaches go beyond all kinds of investigation and reflection; they can only be realized from within. The ultimate meanings are formless, unspeakable; they do not depend on evidence and will not invite controversial arguments. Because the sentient beings have been used to languages and conceptual images for a very long time, they are unable to think and view all dharmas as selfless.

Virtuous Pure Wisdom Great Bodhisattva then said to the Buddha that the ultimate truth is subtle and fathomless; it transcends the sameness and difference of dharma natures and dharma forms; it is very difficult to understand. The Buddha agreed and indicated that some people are ignorant and stubborn, their recognition is limited so they cannot understand the subtle and profound meanings of the ultimate truth. The Buddha then adopted dialectic method and clarified why the ultimate truth is superior to and exceeds the perceived knowledge that is featured with distinction between sameness and difference. The ultimate truth and the knowledge caused by sense perception are neither the same nor different. It is like the white color of the shell: The white color is neither the same as the shell nor different from the shell. It is also like the relationship between the golden color and the gold; they are neither the same nor different. The Buddha became enlightened based on this very subtle and deep meaning of the ultimate truth. After attaining enlightenment, the Buddha has tried his best to teach sentient beings the implied meanings of the ultimate truth.

Well Appearing One conversed with Buddha in the last part of the second chapter. The Buddha concluded their dialogues and said that many sentient beings and dharma practitioners were arrogant and stubborn, always attached to and thus confined by the superficial and narrow knowledge and could not realize the ultimate meanings. The Buddha said that he attained the perfect and universal enlightenment when awakened to the meanings of the ultimate truth, that was subtle, profound, and difficult to understand. Like the formless empty space that permeated all different existent beings (all dharmas) without differentiation but with only one taste and one form, so the ultimate meaning of the truth also permeated all dharmas without differentiation, but with only one taste and one form; namely, formlessness, the Buddha added.

Chapter 3
The forms of the mind consciousness

In chapter 3, the Buddha explained these names and concepts: adana consciousness, alaya consciousness, and mind. He taught how the seeds of the mind interacted with the six spheres: the eye, ear, nose, tongue, body, and conscious spheres.

He pointed out that the sentient beings had reincarnated endlessly in birth and death in the six destinies as heavenly beings, human beings, asuras, animals, hungry ghosts, and hellish beings; they were reborn in physical bodies through eggs, womb, moisture, or transformation.

At the beginning of the birth, the seeds comprised in mind consciousness mature. These seeds reorganize, grow, and expand and hold the material sense roots and their functions, and also hold the forms and the names that are given to perception, differentiation, speech, nonsensical arguments, and disposition.

Another name of this consciousness is adana consciousness since it always follows the physical body and is held by it. It is also called alaya consciousness because this consciousness is absorbed by the physical body; it hides and stays in physical body as long as the body exists. Another name for this consciousness is mind. Why? Because of this consciousness, one's sights, sounds, smells, tastes, and contacts arise and accumulate. They are nurtured by the consciousness to arise and exist in consecutive instants. They appear like reality although they are not. They just arise and extinguish instantaneously. These three names refer to the same essence of life, while each has specific emphasis on one of the mind's functions. When mind consciousness is used, it means that it can perceive the world and the self, and can bring about all kinds of images; these are the phenomena of the world they think they have seen. When adana is used, it provides a ground for all actions and operations. When alaya is used, it means a storage in which all the experiences gained by individuals will be absorbed and stored, from which the karmic effects will be present when the time for retribution is ripe and the conditions are available. In the meantime, the newly obtained experiences will be absorbed and stored in alaya, so it is also called the storage of karmas or the storage of seeds, or the storage of data as we are used to say today. It is an extremely huge storage that can contain informations without limitation. The Buddha pointed out that adana was very thin, subtle, and fathomless; he did not teach this to ignorant ordinary sentient beings because he was afraid that they would differentiate and grasp it as "selfness."

Chapter 4
The forms of all dharmas

In chapter 4, the Buddha summarized three different forms of dharmas (existential beings): universal attachment, dependent origination, and perfect realization.

As provisional names are established to designate particular characteristics of different dharmas, the relevant languages are also created. The holy ones established names and words in order to conveniently teach ordinary sentient beings so that they could learn to distinguish the transient phenomena from the reality. But as people have been used to the provisional names created for transient phenomena for a long time, they will mistake them for real. All dharmas and their phenomena are unreal in the final analysis in terms of ultimate meaning. They are always in change, and the images that we have of them are actually deluded; all existents that appear or sensed by us so lively will finally extinguish once causes and conditions disintegrate. Therefore we will say that the dharmas are neither existent nor nonexistent. To think of the dharmas and their phenomena as real and fixed is the source of vexations, which will inevitably bring about negative karmas, followed by various kinds of suffering. This is how the universal attachment is caused. This attachment to transient impermanent phenomena is so common among ordinary sentient beings; the holy one and his devoted followers have to expediently and skillfully teach and guide the sentient beings to realize the changing dharmas as they really are in order to relieve them from suffering caused by deluded thinking. So the second form of dharmas, the form of dependent origination, is established.

Then what is dependent origination? It means that things arise due to the combination of causes and conditions. None of the beings become existent by itself. Therefore, we may say that the self-nature of all existent beings is dependent arising. As the Buddha says that there is only one form for all dharmas, what he means is that all dharmas are formless; that is, their self-natures are empty. But emptiness does not mean nothing; instead, when causes and conditions combine, the arising of existent beings happen. Where there is arising, there is extinction; as the combination distintegrates, that once existent being will extinguish or become different. Becoming different also means that the original existent dharma is no more existent; it has already distinguished. Therefore arising and extinction of all dharmas in the world is a continuation of incessant changing process. They look as if they were static, but actually they are not. They blind us with illusionary images in our minds.

Once we realize such phenomena of all dharmas in change as they realy are and are no more puzzled by illusions, we enter the perfect realization, the third form of all dharmas. That is, once accepting and realizing this ultimate meaning of emptiness based on the impermanent principle of arising and extinction, the principle of dependent origination, we will be awakened to the realization of all existent beings in the world, then we will understand the realness of equality of all dharmas. The truth that the Buddha intended to convey in this chapter is that all existential beings appear and disappear in front of us following the rule of dependent origination. This is a natural law not created by anyone, but is so as it has always been. Those deluded by the images of the phenomena and incorrectly view them as real and permanent are ignorant. Once insightfully grasping this principle people will be able to attain perfect realization. Therefore, as dependent origination is the only way by which all beings become existent, the universal attachment to the phenomena of all beings as real is a deluded thought based on upside-down understanding. The wise ones will become aware of the reality of dependent origination and attain perfect realization of the world and all existent beings in it.

In Buddhist texts, the existent beings are named dharmas, but the word "dharma" also indicates the rule, the way, or the principle of the truth. Dependent origination is the nature of the phenomena of all dharmas, while perfect realization leads one to the equality of the realness of all dharmas. As the bodhisattvas reflect diligently and reasonably, they will thoroughly understand realness. If they can further cultivate and practice it, they will be able to realize it and finally attain the unsurpassed, perfect, and universal bodhi. The Buddha had used similes in this chapter to make these three forms more understandable.

Chapter 5
The phenomena of selflessness

This chapter begins with the Buddha's reply to Ultimate Meaning Arising Bodhisattva's question. He explained for him the three kinds of selflessness: the form without self-nature, the arising without self-nature, and the ultimate meaning without self-nature.

Ultimate Meaning Arising Great Bodhisattva said that he once thought that the World-Honored One had taught through numberless gates about the aggregates, spheres, dependent origination, four kinds of food, four noble truths, eighteen realms, four bases of mindfulness, four correct endeavors, four bases of power, five roots, five powers, seven factors for enlightenment, and noble eightfold path, including their particular characteristics, their arising and extinction, the permanent termination of vexations and heavy bondages, and their universal knowledge. But on the other hand, Ultimate Meaning Bodhisattva said, he was wondering why the Buddha also said that all dharmas were without self-natures, arising, and extinction and that the dharmas were originally tranquil and their self-natures were in nirvana. So he asked what profound meanings were implied in the Buddha's teachings.

The Thus-Comer replied that it was based on three kinds of selflessness to conclude that all dharmas were without self-natures: Their form is without self-nature, their arising is without self-nature, and their ultimate meaning is without self-nature.

The form without self-nature of all dharmas indicates the reality underlies the universal attachment. It is through the provisionally established names and concepts to recognize the phenomena of all existent beings. The transient phenomena in which all images arise and extinguish incessantly are unreal.

Why is it said that the arising of all dharmas is without self-nature? Because all dharmas arise out of the combination of causes and conditions. They rely on causes and conditions to become existent. They are not intrinsically existent; instead, they are dependently originated. Therefore it is said that their arising is without self-nature.

The truth that all dharmas are dependently originated is named the ultimate meaning of the selflessness of all dharmas. To realize this original pure realness of all dharmas is named the perfect realization of all dharmas. That is the ultimate meaning of all dharmas. The real essence of all dharmas resides firmly in nonaction at all times. The Buddha says that "all dharmas are without selfness is named the ultimate meaning." It is based on this implied meaning that he says that all dharmas do not have arising and extinction; their natures are intrinsically tranquil and inherently in nirvana. Those who do not realize this will have incorrect knowledge and views, which will activate hidden seeds of vexation. Incorrect views and hidden negative seeds work together to make negative karmas and create painful effects in the future. Incessant karma arising will generate endless painful effects. The Buddha taught the three kinds of selflessness expediently and skillfully in order to liberate ordinary sentient beings from incorrect knowledge and views. As in the ultimate-meaning sutras the Buddha had significantly conveyed the message of the three kinds of selflessness, whereas in the non-ultimate-meaning sutras he taught the same message implicitly. The liberation path suggested by the Buddha is not only useful for the learners of the bodhisattva path, but also for the voice-hearer path and self-enlightened one-path pursuers. In the implicit teaching of the non-ultimate-meaning sutras, the learners should pay more attention to the ultimate meanings implied by his words.

Chapter 6
The ultimate meaning of yoga

In this chapter the Buddha and Maitreya Great Bodhisattva had comprehensive and detailed conversations on the practice of concentration (samatha) and investigation or contemplation (vipasyana). In his reply to Maitreya's questions the Buddha taught about the natures and characteristics of samatha and vipasyana. He offered a lot of suggestions useful for what and how the bodhisattvas should learn and cultivate to deal with the difficulties in the progression of stages when working toward the realization of anuttara-samyak-sambodhi.

In the beginning the Buddha said that the bodhisattvas should cultivate samatha and vipasyana of great vehicle by relying on and dwelling in the provisionally established dharma, and never withdraw from the pursuit of anuttara-samyak-sambodhi. The so-called provisionally established dharma for bodhisattvas includes twelve areas of Buddha's teachings: texts (sutra), short verses (geya), prophecy (vyakarana), long verses (gatha), self-statement (udana), origins (nidana), similes (avadana), anecdotes (itivrttaka), past lives (jataka), broad teaching (vaipulya), unusual ways (abdhuta-dharma), and discourses (upadesa). The bodhisattvas should listen to and accept them joyfully, learn to speak of them fluently, reflect on their meanings thoroughly, and develop positive views. They'd better find a quiet place where they can stay alone to reflect on these teachings attentively and uninterruptedly so as to attain freedom and self-ease in body and mind. This is named samatha.

After attaining freedom and self-ease in body and mind, the bodhisattvas will investigate the images appearing in reflection. After attaining superior and definitive understanding, they will get away from the images. In the process the practitioners will think and judge correctly and make comprehensive in-depth investigations with patience; they will recognize and accept with fondness and wise choice in contemplation. This is the approach to mastering vipasyana.

Maitreya Bodhisattva asked the Buddha this question: Are the images produced in samadhi and vipasyana the same as our minds? The Buddha's answer is yes. Why? The images of the perceived objects only reflect what the consciousness of the knowing subject perceives. Therefore all images are just the reflection of our minds. As the mind starts something, images appear. It is like a clean and pure mirror that exactly reflects whatever appears in front of it. To think that the images in the mirror are different from our minds is an upside-down thought.

In responding to Maitreya Bodhisattva's question the Buddha said that in vipasyana one would investigate and reflect on the perceived images, while in samatha one just needed to pay attention to the concentrative mind and keep doing so uninterruptedly.

The Buddha elaborated the three kinds of vipasyana: the vipasyana of perceived images, the vipasyana of general contemplation, and the vipasyana of specific investigation. As three kinds of uninterrupted mind are correspondent with each of the three kinds of vipasyana, there are also three kinds of samatha for each of them. We also have eight kinds of samatha for each of the eight concentrations, from first meditation, second meditation, and so forth, up to the concentration of nonthinking and not nonthinking. In addition, we may have four kinds of samatha for loving-kindness, compassion, joy, and equanimity respectively.

The Buddha said that there were the samatha and vipasyana in accord with the dharmas and the samatha and vipasyana not in accord with the dharmas. The former one means that the bodhisattvas will follow the images of the dharmas they have received or they have thought of to contemplate their meanings. The latter one means that the bodhisattvas will follow the meanings given by others to contemplate. They will investigate, for instance, such statements as "all dharmas are always in change," "all actions bring about suffering," "all dharmas are without selfness," or "tranquility in nirvana in the final analysis." The former one is for the sharp learners, while the latter one is for the slow learners. The Buddha also pointed out how the samatha vipasyana based on general approach was different from the samatha vipasyana based on particular approach. Those who follow the particular approach will cultivate samatha vipasyana based on individual sutras, while the general approach practitioners will put all sutras together and make them a system and contemplate it attentively. The general approach has three different kinds: minor general approach, major general approach, and numberless general approach. The minor general approach will merge all sutras and treatises and so forth of one of the twelve teaching areas into one system and reflect on it attentively. The major general approach will put all sutras and so forth in all areas of Buddha's teachings as one system and reflect on it attentively. The numberless general approach will put numberless dharma teachings given by Thus-Comer, numberless dharma words and sentences, and numberless denoted and connoted meanings in interpretations together as a system and contemplate it attentively.

The Buddha suggested five criteria to tell if the practitioners have attained samatha vipasyana based on general approach. The first is that when undertaking reflection, the practitioners will feel the seeds on which heavy vexations rely melt away in every single instant. The second is the practitioners will enjoy dharma joy. The third is they will experience immeasurable rays of light coming from ten directions without differentiation. The fourth is that they will purify what they have intended in cultivation, and indifferentiated images will appear in front of them. The fifth is that they will receive and absorb superior effects that will turn into superior causes afterward so as to fulfill dharma body.

The Buddha instructed that if the pratitioners' minds are flying very high or if they are afraid of being so, they may think of the things with which they are disgusted or the things they dislike in order to calm themselves down. This is named calming down. When their minds are sinking or drowned in anxieties or vexations, they may think of pleasant things or some inspiring ideas so as to draw themselves back to tranquility. This is named the form of raising spirits. If they have practiced samatha, vipasyana, or both and are disturbed by defilements, they may try to stay away from deliberate intention for a while, or just let their thoughts go. This is named the form of renunciation.

Maitreya Bodhisattva asked what "knowing dharmas" and "knowing meanings" are. The Buddha replied that knowing dharmas means the bodhisattvas know the names, the sentences, the texts, the particular characteristics of the perceived objects, and the common characteristics of the perceived objects. "Knowing meanings" means to know ten things.

1. Knowing all kinds of contaminated and pure dharmas, such as the five aggregates, six inner spheres, six outer spheres, and so forth.

2. Knowing the realness of all contaminated and pure dharmas. In this category seven kinds of realness are listed:

   1) The realness of drifting: All actions or phenomena just arise and extinguish; they are without selfness; they do not really occure in the three phases of time; temporality is not real nor existent.

   2) The realness of forms or phenomena: All phenomena as well as individual sentient beings do not have ego or selfness.

   3) The realness of cognition: All phenomena or images are just the reflection or impression of our mind consciousness.

   4) The realness of establishment: The noble truth of suffering as taught by the Buddha.

   5) The realness of negative karmas: The noble truth of the cause of suffering as taught by the Buddha.

   6) The realness of purification: The noble truth of the cessation of suffering as taught by the Buddha.

   7) The realness of the path: The noble truth of the path for the cessation of suffering as taught by the Buddha.

3. Knowing the perceiving subject: the six inner spheres,

namely, the eye, ear, nose, tongue, body, and conscious spheres.

4. Knowing the perceived objects: the sight, sound, smell, taste, touch, and mental images. The inner six spheres may also become the perceived objects when they are under investigation; a kind of self-reflection.

5. Knowing the established world: the establishment of the physical world, in which various realms of sentient being and insentient being are also established.

6. Knowing the meaning of using living supplies.

7. Knowing the upside-down thoughts and incorrect views: For instance, mistaking impermanence for permanence, pains for pleasures, impurity for purity, and selflessness for self-nature.

8. The thoughts and views contrary to the upside-down ones; in addition, knowing how to deal with and correct the upside-down thoughts and views.

9. Knowing the contaminated vexations, contaminated karma, and contaminated arising.

10. Knowing all bodhi factors that help people get out of contamination.

The Buddha said that the bodhisattvas who have learned to know the following five kinds of meanings are also named "knowing meanings."

1. The first is knowing the things comprehensively. Name-

ly, they know various aggregates, various inner spheres, various outer spheres, and so forth.

2. The second is knowing the meanings comprehensively. Namely, the bodhisattvas know all kinds of phenomena that they should know. They should know the world; the superior ultimate meanings; merits and virtues; faults; conditions; phases of time; the circulation of arising, duration, and decay; illness; causes of suffering; realness; reality; dharma realm; broad and brief teachings; giving answers definitively and clearly; clarifying the meanings before answering properly and separately; giving teachings in implicit and secret way; giving teachings in explicit way; and so forth.

3. The third is knowing the causes comprehensively. The bodhisattvas should know the bodhi factors leading ones to know the things and the meanings mentioned above comprehensively.

4. The fourth is knowing the effects comprehensively. They should know the effects resulted from the cultivation of voice-hearer dharma, bodhisattva dharma, and so forth.

5. The fifth is knowing what to do after realizing enlightenment. That is, they should teach the perfect knowledge of liberation and propogate and lecture on it widely.

Furthermore, those who know the following four kinds of meanings are also named "knowing meanings," the Buddha said.

1. The first is knowing that the mind can hold and store all kinds of seeds; it can continue to receive and absorb new seeds.

2. The second is knowing that the mind can receive stimuli and bring about various kinds of feelings.

3. The third is knowing that the mind cannot only perceive, but also differentiate, reason, analyze, judge, and make all kinds of decisions.

4. The fourth is knowing the meanings of contamination and purification or purity.

Furthermore, the Buddha said that those who know the following three kinds of meanings are also named "knowing meanings."

1. Knowing the names, words, sentences, and the combination of sentences.

2. Knowing the meanings of meanings. There are ten kinds in this category:

   1) knowing the reality
   2) knowing the comprehensive knowledge
   3) knowing permanent termination
   4) knowing realization
   5) knowing cultivation and learning
   6) knowing the differences among the five kinds of knowing meanings mentioned above
   7) knowing the interaction and relationship between perceiving subject and perceived objects

8) knowing the obstacles hindering comprehensive knowledge

9) knowing the factors compliant with the dharma

10) knowing the faults of incomprehensive knowledge and the merits of comprehensive knowledge

3. Knowing the realms. There are five kinds of this knowledge:

1) knowing the physical world

2) knowing the realm of sentient beings

3) knowing the dharma realm; namely, the realm of the dharmas perceived.

4) knowing the ones who are taught and guided

5) knowing the expedient and skillful ways applied for taming and guiding

The Buddha explained the differences among three ways of forming wisdom: through hearing, thinking, and the cultivation of samatha and vipasyana. The wisdom formed through hearing means the practitioners only rely on what they heard; so they are confined to the surface meanings of what they heard. It will be good if they can go further beyond that. So the wisdom formed through thinking will lead ones to go beyond what they are told so as to grasp the underlying meanings. The practitioners who learn through the cultivation of samatha and vipasyana will either rely on or not rely on texts and hearing; they can realize the essential meanings well and understand the surface and the underlying meanings. As the images appearing in samadhi interact harmoniously with the objects that the practitioners see and investigate, the reality will appear as it really is and the practitioners will be able to realize liberation.

Maitreya Bodhisattva again raised the questions: What is intelligence? What is viewpoint? The Buddha explained that intelligence is the exquisite wisdom produced by practicing samatha and vipasyana based on general approach; while viewpoint is the exquisite wisdom produced by practicing samatha and vipasyana based on particular approach.

What kinds of images should be cast off? And how/when cultivating samatha and vipasyana? The Buddha said, being attentive to realness will help ones cast off the images of the dharmas and the images of meanings. This means that when undertaking cultivation, the bodhisattvas should not rely on or try to attain something, nor should they contemplate the phenomena or images of various dharma realms. Should realness be cast off also? The Buddha replied that as realness is already free from reliance and attainment, why should it be cast off? The Buddha said that people cannot see their faces clearly and accurately in turbid water or in front of an unclean mirror, so we cannot see the realness of dharmas until we have cleaned and purified our minds. Three ways were suggested by the Buddha to see our own minds: hearing the correct dharma, reflecting on the truth, and practicing the truth.

Maitreya Bodhisattva asked again, "When cultivating diligently, what kinds of images are difficult to cast off but should be cast off by the bodhisattvas who have known the dharmas and meanings? And how?" The Buddha replied that there are ten kinds of images haunting bodhisattvas that should be cast off. They can be cast off by various kinds of emptiness.

1.   The images of words and sentences caused by knowing

dharmas and meanings should be cast off. They can be cast off by emptiness of all dharmas.

2. The images of the drifting of arising, extinction, duration, and decay caused by knowing the realness of establishment should be cast off. They can be cast off by emptiness of formlessness and emptiness of nontemporality.

3. The images of attachment to body and self-conceit caused by knowing the perceiving subject should be cast off. They can be cast off by emptiness of internal emptiness and emptiness of nonattainment.

4. The images of grasping and attachment to property caused by knowing the meaning of what they have gained should be cast off. They can be cast off by external emptiness.

5. The images of inner comfort and ease as well as the images of outer exquisiteness and purity caused by knowing the meaning of receiving and enjoying living supplies and human services should be cast off. They can be cast off by internal-external emptiness and emptiness of original nature.

6. Numberless images caused by knowing the meaning of establishment should be cast off. They can be cast off by emptiness of space.

7. Images of inner tranquility and liberation caused by knowing formlessness should be cast off. They can be cast off by emptiness of conditioned phenomena.

8. The selfless images of individual sentient beings, the images of selfless dharmas, the images of consciousness only, and the images of superior ultimate meaning caused by knowing the realness of images should be cast off. They can be cast off by emptiness in the final analysis, emptiness of selflessness, emptiness of selfless self-nature, and emptiness of ultimate meaning.

9. The images of unconditioned reality and the images of changelessness caused by knowing the pure realness should be cast off. They can be cast off by emptiness of unconditioned reality and emptiness of changelessness.

10. The images of emptiness caused by attentive reflection on dealing with emptiness should be cast off. They can be cast off by emptiness of emptiness.

When these ten kinds of images are removed, all images the practitioners have in samadhi will be removed. They will become free from the siege of contaminated images.

Maitreya Bodhisattva asked the Buddha again, "What is the general nature of emptiness in which the bodhisattvas should not get lost?" The Buddha was pleased to hear this question, and said that to stay far away from universal attachment to various pure and impure images in dependent origination and in perfect realization without attainment is the general nature of emptiness. Once losing this general nature of emptiness, one will also lose great vehicle. He also said that the correct views caused by pure precepts, hearing, and thinking are the causes of samatha vipasyana. The virtuous and pure mind and the virtuous and pure wisdom, as well as all virtuous dharmas of voice-hearers and Thus-Comers, are the effects of samatha vipasyana. The karma of samatha vipasyana is to get rid of two bondages: the bondage of deluded images and the bondage of heavy vexations.

The Buddha pointed out that five bonds will hinder samatha, vipasyana, or both. Being attached to body and property is the obstacle for learning samatha. Inability and unwillingness to learn and follow the sages' teachings will hinder the cultivation of vipasyana. Indulging in images, residing in impurity, and being easily satisfied with minor achievement will hinder both.

The Buddha further pointed out that five coverings will also hinder samatha, vipasyana, or both. The covering of restless mind and regret will hinder the cultivation of samatha. The covering of stupor and sleepiness and the covering of doubt will hinder the cultivation of vipasyana. The covering of greedy desire and the covering of hatred and anger will hinder both. When the practitioners have not only eliminated restlessness of mind and repentance, but also stupor and sleepiness, they are named fulfilling the pure samatha path. When they have not only eliminated stupor, sleepiness, and doubt, but also the restlessness of mind and repentance, they are named fulfilling the pure vipasyana path.

The Buddha cautioned the practitioners that they should be aware of five kinds of unstable and unconcentrated mind that goes astray when undertaking samatha and vipasyana. They are:

1. The intention instability, namely, the intention goes astray: the mind with great vehicle aspiration turns to look after voice-hearer vehicle or self-enlightened one vehicle.

2. The outer instability, namely, the outer mind goes astray: the mind chasing five-sense desires is contaminated in their reflections on outer world.

3. The inner mind that goes astray: The mind becomes dull, sleepy, or sinking or becomes fond of and immersed in the state of samapatti; or the mind is contaminated by associated vexations related to samapatti.

4. The instability of mind caused by phenomena: If they pay attention to images derived from outside world and deliberately think of them in samadhi, then they will have unstable mind caused by images.

5. The instability of mind caused by heavy afflictions: If one's intention and cognition give rise to various feelings, and due to this person's heavy defiled disposition, ego and arrogance will be activated.

Maitreya Bodhisattva asked the World-Honored One again, "In each stage, from the first stage of bodhisattva up to the eleventh stage of Thus-Comer, what obstacles can be dealt with and removed by samatha and vipasyana?" As to this crucial question, the Buddha elucidated in detail with great patience.

1. In the first stage, the obstacles of the three kinds of contamination, namely, the contamination of vexations, the contamination of karma, and the contamination of arising caused by inferior destinies can be dealt with and removed.

2. In the second stage, the obstacle of presently occurring

subtle violation of precepts can be dealt with and re-moved.

3. In the third stage, the obstacle produced by greedy de-sires can be dealt with and removed.

4. In the fourth stage, the obstacle of attachment to concentration and attachment to dharma can be dealt with and removed.

5. In the fifth stage, the obstacle of aspiring to nirvana but turning away from birth and death can be dealt with and removed.

6. In the sixth stage, the obstacle of lots of presently continuing images of differentiation can be dealt with and removed.

7. In the seventh stage, the obstacle of presently happening subtle and very thin images can be dealt with and removed.

8. In the eighth stage, the obstacle of making effort deliberately on formlessness and the obstacle of the feeling not comfortable about form can be dealt with and removed.

9. In the ninth stage, the obstacle of not being able to speak expedient and skillful words freely and at ease can be dealt with and removed.

10. In the tenth stage, the obstacle of not being able to realize perfect dharma body can be dealt with and removed.

11. In the stage of Thus-Comer, the obstacle of extremely

subtle and subtlest vexations and the obstacle caused by what one has known can be dealt with and removed.

Because all these obstacles are finally removed, the practitioners of bodhisattva path are able to realize all kinds of perfect knowledge and correct views and will have no attainment and hindrance any more. It is based on this fulfillment the bodhisattva-path practitioners will build up the uppermost and purest dharma body.

As the bodhisattvas become familiar with samatha and vipasyana, they will be able to correctly reflect on what they have heard or what they have thought of based on the seven kinds of realness through superior concentration to discard the very thin and subtle images, not to mention the coarse ones. Then they will have quick access to the knowledge of seven kinds of realness and are ready to cultivate their minds by dealing with all bonds, coverings, and restlessness, see the path of the truth, and enter onto the bodhisattva path of nonarising. Now they are reborn in the family of Thus-Comer. They will further progress to higher levels, remove all images and heavy vexations, and forge their minds like forging gold. They will move forward to realize and attain anuttara-samyak-sambodhi upon completion of all necessary practices. This is how the bodhisattvas realize and attain the unsurpassed, perfect, and universal bodhi through the cultivation of samatha and vipasyana.

The so-called thin and subtle images of mind mentioned above are

1.   the images of what the mind grasps and holds;

2. the images of what the mind perceives;

3. the contaminated and pure images;

4. the inner images;

5. the outer images;

6. the images caused by thinking; for instance, that "I should cultivate all dharmas beneficial for sentient being";

7. the images produced when thinking of the correct knowledge;

8. the images produced when thinking of realness;

9. the images produced when thinking of the four noble truths;

10. the images produced when thinking of the arising, duration, decay, and extinction of the conditioned dharmas;

11. the images produced when thinking of the unconditioned dharmas that are without arising, duration, decay, and extinction;

12. the images produced when thinking of permanence;

13. the images produced when thinking of impermanence;

14. the images produced when thinking of the suffering of change;

15. the images produced when thinking of the suffering of changelessness;

16. the images produced when thinking of the particular characteristics of the conditioned dharmas;

17. the images produced when thinking of the common characteristics of the conditioned dharmas;

18. the images of the dharmas produced when knowing all dharmas;

19. the images produced in an attempt to remove the images of selflessness of individual sentient beings and the images of selflessness of existent beings; and

20. the images produced in trying to cultivate and deal with all bonds, coverings, and unstable minds.

All these are the fine and subtle images of the mind that should be discarded when undertaking correct reflection.

As Maitreya Bodhisattva asked what kinds of cultivation will elicit broad and great authority and virtues of bodhisattvas, the Buddha replied that knowing well the six spheres will make this elicitation possible.

1. Knowing well the sixteen different ways of mind arising.

    1) The arising of the unintelligible consciousness named adana, that will delude people and make them believe that the physical world is solid and stable.

    2) The arising of the sixth consciousness as perceiving subject.

    3) The arising of the shallow mental images in the realm of desire.

4) The arising of the broad mental images in the realm of form.

5) The arising of the numberless mental images in the boundless emptiness and boundless consciousness in the realm of formlessness.

6) The arising of the subtle mental images in the sphere of nothingness in the realm of formlessness.

7) The arising of the faraway mental images in the sphere of nonthinking and not nonthinking in the realm of formlessness.

8) The arising of the mental images caused by flawless consciousness and the concentration of extinction beyond the world.

9) The arising of the mental images correspondent with the suffering in the hells.

10) The arising of the mental images caused by various feelings correspondent with the realm of desire.

11) The arising of the mental images caused by delight correspondent with the first and second meditations.

12) The arising of the mental images caused by joy correspondent with the third meditation.

13) The arising of the mental images caused by the feeling of renunciation correspondent with the fourth meditation and so forth and the concentration of nonthinking and not nonthinking.

14) The arising of the contaminated images correspondent with the major vexations such as greediness, hatred and anger, ignorance, arrogance, skepticism, and incorrect views and the associated minor vexations.

15) The arising of the pure images correspondent with the

virtuous dharmas such as belief, shame, confession of wrongdoing, no greed, no hatred, no ignorance, diligence, relaxation and self-ease, self-restraint, equanimity, harmlessness, and so forth.

16) The arising of the neutral images not correspondent with the virtuous or the not virtuous dharmas.

2. Knowing well how the mind resides. Namely, knowing the realness of cognition as merely the reflection of the mind consciousness.

3. Knowing well how the mind gets out of the bondages, the bondage of the images of dharmas and the bondage of heavy vexations caused by disposition, karmic obstacles, hidden seeds of vexations, and so forth.

4. Knowing that the mind power will increase as the hindrances caused by the bondage of forms and the bondage of heavy vexations increase.

5. Knowing that the mind power will decrease as the hindrances caused by the bondage of forms and the bondage of heavy vexations decrease.

6. Knowing well the eight liberations, eight vexation-overcoming meditations, and ten universal contemplations and how one will cultivate them and cast off what should be removed.

In the final portion of the conversation, the Buddha explained to Maitreya Bodhisattva the difference between the nirvana without remainder and the nirvana with remainder. He said that two kinds of feelings would extinguish permanently upon the realization of nirvana without remainder: the heavy feelings caused and experienced by one's own body and the feelings produced by the interaction between people and the world. Four heavy feelings of body were mentioned by the Buddha: the feelings experienced by the five sense organs; the feelings experienced by the mind consciousness; the feelings caused by the mature karmic effects occurring in the present; the feelings caused by the immature karmic effects that will occur in the future. Four heavy feelings caused by interaction between people and the world were also mentioned: the heavy feelings derived from the world that people rely on; the heavy feelings derived from living supplies; the heavy feelings caused by using living supplies; and the heavy feelings caused by the attachment to the world and all sentient and insentient beings in the world. All these feelings will extinguish permanently when one enters into nirvana without remainder.

The Buddha further explained that for the ones entering into the nirvana without remainder, all their feelings have extinguished permanently. While for the ones entering into nirvana with remainder, their karmic effects are not mature yet and their feelings remain active, but because their feelings have become pure and flawless, their heavy bondages and vexations have also disappeared forever.

This chapter contains the perfect, purest, and most exquisite path of yoga that the Buddha teaches.

Chapter 7
The ultimate meaning of the stages of paramita

In this chapter the conversations between Buddha and

Viewing-in-Freedom Bodhisattva about bodhisattva-path cultivation were recorded. Viewing-in-Freedom Bodhisattva asked Buddha various kinds of questions in this regard, and the Buddha replied to his questions thoroughly that a down-to-earth guideline of bodhisattva-path cultivation was clearly manifested for the great-vehicle practitioners.

In the beginning the Buddha depicted the characteristics of the ten stages of bodhisattva cultivation. As the practitioners learn and progress from the first stage of ecstasy, the second of freedom from defilements, and so forth, through the highest level of Buddhahood, they should get to know the merits and the weaknesses that they may encounter in each stage and what they should do to deal with and overcome the difficulties.

The Buddha explained why the first stage of bodhisattva cultivation is named "the stage of ecstasy," the second stage is named "the stage of freedom from defilements," the third stage is named "the stage of emitting light," and so forth. The Buddha has established the ten stages of cultivation for bodhisattvas owing to the fact that twenty-two kinds of ignorance and eleven kinds of heavy bondages may appear in these stages that should be dealt with. The Buddha urged the bodhisattvas to break through the network of ignorance and walk bravely across the heavy dark forests so as to realize and attain anuttara-samyak-saṃbodhi.

The Buddha indicated eight kinds of purity that happen in all stages in order to encourage the bodhisattva-path practitioners and strengthen their confidence: the purity of motivation; the purity of the mind in concentration; the purity of compassion; the purity of learning the six paramitas to cross the river to the other shore; the purity of paying respect to, making offerings to, and serving the Buddhas; the purity of assisting the sentient beings to mature; the purity of birth; and the purity of accomplishing the merits, virtues, dignity, and demeanors of the bodhisattva.

The birth of the bodhisattva in the world is the most unique and superior thing of all births because it is the result of the accumulation of the extremely pure virtuous roots caused by the wise choices and the merciful and compassionate vows to delivering all sentient beings and purifying their defilements.

The Buddha said that the bodhisattvas should learn giving, precept, forbearance, diligence, meditation, and wisdom paramitas. Paramita means perfection; it also means to ferry over from this shore of vexations to the other shore of liberation. Five approaches for practicing the six paramitas were suggested: deeply believe and understand the exquisite and subtle correct teachings correspondent with the paramita; diligently cultivate the ten actions with the exquisite knowledge developed through hearing, reflection, and cultivation; protect the bodhi mind all the time; stay close to the real, virtuous intellectuals; and cultivate the virtuous dharmas incessantly. The learning of the six paramitas can overcome and remove various vexations, so the bodhisattvas as the learners of paramita will become superior and do things beneficial for all sentient beings. Four more paramitas: expedient sillfulness, aspiration, power, and knowledge paramitas are established as aids to the fulfillment of the six paramitas. The Buddha cautioned bodhisattvas of the six things contrary to paramita. He further said that if the bodhisattvas are satisfied with merely giving money and materials without teaching receivers to stay away from the not virtuous actions and turn to the virtuous actions, they are not practicing the expedient giving. The real benefits, he reminded the bodhisattva-path practitioners, come from establishing sentient beings in virtuous dharmas.

The Buddha said that paramita is so named because of five reasons: (1) Paramita is free from defilements; it is not contaminated by the things contrary to paramita. (2) Paramita is free from attachment and craving; it is not attached to the desirable effects derived from practicing paramita. (3) Paramita is free from guilt; it works diligently not apart from compassion, reasonable way, constancy, and sincerity. (4) Paramita is free from differentiation; it is not attached to particular characteristics of dharmas. (5) Paramita is always with a correct destination of transference, the unsurpassed bodhi.

Because paramita is free from contamination, the bodhisattvas are able to cultivate paramitas constantly, sincerely, diligently in present life. Because paramita is free from attachment and craving, the bodhisattvas are able to absorb the factors of self-restraint as the causes for the effects of cultivation to come in the future. Because paramita is free from guilt, the bodhisattvas will do nothing wrong, and are able to cultivate and learn paramita in an extremely perfect, pure, and virtuous way. Because paramita is free from differentiation, the bodhisattvas are able to fulfill expedient and skillful paramita quickly. Because of the correct transference, the bodhisattvas will enjoy paramita and its desirable effects unexhaustedly wherever they are reborn until attaining the unsurpassed bodhi.

The Buddha said that there were six things that the great vehicle practitioners should be admonished when cultivating the six paramitas: they should not view desires, wealth, pleasure, and self-ease as merits and superior benefits; they should not view what one does, speaks, and thinks without self-restraint as merits and superior benefits; they should not view intolerance and looking down on others with contempt as merits and superior benefits; they should not view laziness and indulgence in desire pleasures as merits and superior benefits; they should not view defiled actions in chaotic environment as merits and superior benefits; and they should not view seeing, hearing, knowing, and speaking nonsensical arguments as merits and superior benefits.

There are also seven kinds of purity for all paramitas in general. They are: (1) when practicing paramita, the bodhisattvas do no care whether others know them or not. (2) They are not attached to various dharmas. (3) They are not puzzled about what they are doing; so they will not ask this question: Will I attain the great bodhi? (4) They will not boast about their own achievements and look down on others. (5) They will not be arrogant and without self-restraint. (6) They will not be easily satisfied with minor achievement in learning and cultivation. (7) They will not be reluctant to teach others the correct dharma or become jealous.

For practicing the six paramitas, the Buddha taught seven particular pure forms for each paramita. There are seven pure forms for practicing giving paramita: practicing giving with pure things; practicing giving with pure actions in accord with pure precept; practicing giving with pure views; practicing giving with pure mind; practicing giving with pure words; practicing giving with pure wisdom; and purifying defilements before practicing giving.

For pure-precept paramita, the seven pure forms are: knowing well how and why all precepts, rules, laws, rituals, and demeanors are established; knowing well how to get out of violation of precepts properly; observing precepts at all times; dwelling firmly in precepts; behaving in accord with precepts at all times; knowing well how to make amends and correct wrongdoings when doing something wrong; and learning all kinds of precepts, rules, laws, rituals, and demeanors.

When practicing forbearance, the bodhisattvas should stay with seven kinds of purity. (1) They should deeply believe that one's own karmic effects will finally mature at different times and in different ways; therefore, when undesirable things happen to them, they should not complain, get angry, scold back to, fight back to, threaten, or play tricks on others. (2) They should not do harm to others. (3) They should not stay in hatred. (4) They should not offend others when giving them advice. (5) They should try to solve problems actively before becoming worse. (6) They should not keep silent only because they are threatened or because of greedy desire. (7) They should continue to help others by giving advice even if they have done once.

When practicing diligence, the bodhisattvas should stay with seven kinds of purity. (1) They fully understand the nature of equality in practicing diligence. (2) They do not exaggerate their own strengths or dispise others when practicing diligence bravely. (3) They will learn to possess great power and authority. (4) They will move forward powerfully. (5) They learn to become capable of overcoming difficulties. (6) They are resolute, brave, and vigorous. (7) They will never stay away from various virtuous dharmas.

When practicing meditation, the bodhisattvas should stay with seven kinds of purity. (1) They can master the images in meditation well. (2) They can fulfill the realness of samadhi well.

(3) They can master different kinds of samadhi, the worldly and the ultimate, simultaneously. (4) They can master samatha and vipasyana freely. (5) They can master the samadhi of emptiness, formlessness, and nonaspiration freely. (6) They can practice the samadhi of the eight liberations, eight vexation-overcoming meditations, nine concentrations in sequence, and ten universal contemplations freely. (7) They can cultivate and learn numberless samadhi based on hearing texts of bodhisattva path.

When practicing wisdom, the bodhisattvas should stay with seven kinds of purity. (1) They will stay away from two extremes but stay on middle path. (2) Because of wisdom, they can realize the liberation gates of emptiness, formlessness, and nonaspiration as they really are. (3) They will realize three kinds of nature: the nature of universal attachment, the nature of dependet origination, and the nature of perfect actualization as they really are; namely, their natures are without selfness. (4) They will realize the three kinds of selflessness: the selflessness of images, the selflessness of arising, and the selflessness of ultimate meaning as they really are. (5) They will realize the meanings of the five kinds of worldly learning: language and literature, technology, medicine, logic, and inner learning (religious, spiritual, and philosophical) as they really are. (6) They will realize the ultimate meanings, namely, the seven kinds of realness, as they really are. The seven kinds of realness teach us: the realness of drifting is that all actions and phenomena of arising and extinction are without selfness, and the temporality is unreal and nonexistent; the realness of phenomena is that all individuals and phenomena are selfless; the realness of cognition is that all images are just the reflection or impression of mind consciousness; the realness of establishment is the noble truth of suffering as taught by the Buddha; the realness of negative karmas is the noble truth of the cause of suffering as taught by the Buddha; the realness of purification is the noble truth of the cessation of suffering as taught by the Buddha; and the realness of the path is the noble truth of the path for the cessation of suffering as taught by the Budda. (7) Because of nondifferentiation, staying away from various nonsensical arguments, dwelling in pure unified essential meaning, and taking care of numberless general perspectives of dharma, and also because of vipasyana, the bodhisarrvas are able to accomplish the cultivation in accord with correct dharma.

Besides, there are four most superior authorities and virtues that are shared by all six paramitas: The bodhisattvas will stay away from stinginess, violation of precepts, hatred, laziness, restlessness, and incorrect views; will be prepared for the unsurpassed, perfect, and universal bodhi; will absorb present dharmas to benefit sentient beings; and attain broad, great, and unexhausted positive effects.

The Buddha further pointed out that great compassion is the cause of all paramitas; the exquisite, subtle, and desirable effects beneficial for all sentient beings are the results of the paramitas; and the perfect, unsurpassed, broad, and great bodhi is the grand justice and benefit of all paramitas.

Responding to Viewing-in-Freedom Bodhisattva's question, the Buddha said that the broadest and greatest paramitas are those with correct transference but without pollution, attachment, and craving. The brightest paramitas are those without guilt and differention but with unpolluted wise choice and decision. The unmovable paramitas are those that have entered the stage of nonregression. And the purest paramitas are those absorbed in the tenth stage and the stage of Buddhahood.

As to the question: "Why as the desirable effects gained by the bodhisattvas are unexhausted, so paramita is also unexhausted?" The Buddha said that it is because the desirable effects will turn into the causes for the effects to come in the future and generate more and more cultivations of paramitas. As this starts, such a succession will continue uninterruptedly and endlessly.

Because paramitas always play as powerful causes for bringing ecstasy, bringing benefits for oneself and others in the final analysis, producing desirable effects in the future, removing all kinds of defilements, and bringing about perfect tranquil and peaceful nirvana, the bodhisattvas deeply believe in and love paramitas. The Buddha added.

"As the bodhisattvas can absorb living supplies of the world and are capable and compassionate, why are there so many sentient beings still living in poverty with extremely painful situations?" As to this question, the Buddha said that it is because of the negative karmas of the sentient beings that make them suffer. Like the extremely thirsty ghosts who can see the ocean, but when they get close to the waters, the ocean will dry up immediately. If the bodhisattvas just give food and living supplies without teaching correct dharma, the ordinary sentient beings will not really change their destinies; what they really need is the fundamental change of thoughts and views.

In the final portion of the chapter, the Buddha clarifies the relationship between the voice-hearer vehicle and the great vehicle. Although he taught the five aggregates, six inner spheres, outer spheres, and so forth for voice-hearer vehicle, he had never said that the nature of voice-hearer vehicle is different from that of great vehicle. The Buddha said, he had taught that all dharmas shared the same dharma realm and essential meaning, but some persons misunderstood what he said and added something to and took something from what he really taught. These persons had suggested meanings not implied by him. They even stressed that the voice-hearer vehicle and the great vehicle were in conflict, thus people began to argue against each other endlessly. He said that there was only one vehicle. This is the meaning implied by his teachings.

Chapter 8
The things fulfilled by the Thus-Comer

In this chapter the Buddha replied to Manjusri's question about the dharma body and the retribution body of the Thus-Comer. The Thus-Comer's retribution body was demonstrated by his whole life in this world, beginning with his birth, the education he received, and his marriage and family life. Then he renounced the position of king and left his family. First he lived an ascetic life as a way of cultivation. As he found that the practice based on torturing one's physical body had nothing to do with enlightenment and liberation, he modified his way and converted to middle path. The right path led him to the realization of the unsurpassed bodhi, become a Buddha, and begin the career of widely propagating the correct dharma he discovered to benefit all sentient beings until entering nirvana.

The Buddha made detailed description of the contents and learning methods of the three major parts of his dharma teaching: sutra, vinaya, and matrka. What is sutra? The Buddha said that he absorbed all the things here and now and used them to reveal various dharmas of the world for sentient beings. These are the contents of sutra. It seems that the sutra thus consists of myriads of things in the world. But the Buddha had focused on four categories for the truth aspirants: the things about hearing correct teachings, the things the practitioners will aspire to, the things about cultivation and learning, and the things about the attainment of the bodhi.

The sutra can also be divided into nine things. What are they? They are (1) the establishment of the sentient beings; (2) the things about the six inner spheres that receive stimuli from the six outer spheres and thus form the twelve spheres; (3) the things about the twelve chains of dependent origination; (4) the things about the four kinds of food for nurturing sentient beings; (5) the things about contamination and purification: the four noble truths; (6) the things about the differences of numberless dharma realms; (7) the things about the ones who teach the correct dharma: the Buddha and his disciples; (8) the things about what taught by the Buddha; and (9) the things about assemblies and the audiences in assemblies.

The sutra can also be divided into twenty-nine things. Among them four are the contaminated things that will produce karmic effects of vexations. They are (1) the phenomena of the conditioned dharmas; (2) the conditioned dharmas that are drifting in sequence; (3) the attachment to the selfness of individuals that serves as the cause of reincarnation in the lives to come; and (4) the attachment to the features of the dharmas that serves as the cause of reincarnation in the lives to come.

There are twenty-five pure things in sutra. The first four things belong to the world and are in accord with the correct worldly dharma. They are (1) staying in correct mindfulness of correct dharma after hearing the dharma; (2) reflecting on the correct dharma diligently; (3) letting the mind dwell peacefully in correct dharma; and (4) letting the mind dwell joyfully in meditation and enjoy the worldly dharmas that are appearing presently. The following pure things belong to the world beyond. They are (5) the expedient way of contemplating the four noble truths to transcend the flawed causes and conditions of the suffering in the three realms; (6) knowing comprehensively the noble truth of suffering; (7) undertaking cultivation in order to cease the cause of suffering; (8) realizing nirvana in order to cease suffering; (9) practicing the path for the cessation of suffering; (10) no regression in cultivation after seeing the path; (11) the things about mental images; (12) the things about the sixteen kinds of images perceived when contemplating the four noble truths in the realm of desire and in the (upper) realms of form and formlessness; (13) the things about skillful contemplation of the vexations terminated and the vexations not yet terminated; (14) the things about the restless and chaotic things; (15) the concentrations that make the minds not restless; (16) the things about the basis the steady mind relies on; (17) the things about diligent cultivation with additional efforts so as to progress step by step; (18) the things about the superior benefits gained from cultivation and learning; (19) the things about the solid and stable effects of cultivation; (20) the things about holy ones' great actions; (21) the blessings and wisdom caused by holy actions; (22) the thorough and insightful understanding of the reality; (23) the realization of nirvana; (24) the correct views of the world derived from learning vinaya taught well by the Buddha that are superior to all views of other paths;

and (25) the things about regression as staying away from cultivation.

The second category of teaching given by the Buddha is vinaya. That is moral education and law education. It appears in a form that looks as confining one's actions by following a set of rules while its essence is observance based on inner self-reflection with free will and flexibility in daily practice. So the aim of vinaya is self-liberation instead of imprisonment. The Buddha said to Manjusri Bodhisattva that precept was meant by the dharmas correspondent with individual liberation that he had demonstrated and explained for the dharma practitioners, including the voice-hearers and bodhisattvas. He said there were seven forms of vinaya: (1) the teaching about the rules and rituals that bodhisattvas should observe; (2) the teaching about the four crucial laws that the bodhisattvas must not violate so that they can become extraordinary or superior; (3) the teaching about the violation of precept; (4) the teaching about the features of the practitioners who incline to violate rules; (5) the teaching about the features of the practitioners who do not violate rules; (6) the teaching about repentance; and (7) the teaching about discarding the rules and rituals.

What are the four crucial laws? They are: the bodhisattvas should not boast about themselves and slander others; they should not save the correct dharma and property for themselves without sharing them with others; they should not get angry and stay in hatred; and they should not slander the bodhisattva-path texts.

The third category of Buddha's teaching is matrka, the category of treatise. The Buddha said that he used eleven forms to reveal and expound various dharmas. What are the eleven forms? They are:

1) The form of the world, including the teaching of the individuals in reincarnation, the teaching of the features of universal attachment, and the teaching of the karmic causes and effects of the operations of all dharmas.

2) The form of the ultimate meaning that comprises seven kinds of realness.

3) The form of the teaching in accord with the factors for enlightenment that should be known comprehensively.

4) The form of the transient beings. This indicates the teaching about the contemplation of the mental images of various dharmas in eight areas: the contemplation of the reality, the establishments, the faults, the merits and virtues, the essential meanings, the drifting, the principles, and the phenomena of all beings, either from the general perspective or from the particular perspective.

(4-1) The reality is the realness of all dharmas.

(4-2) The establishments are the establishment of the individuals in reincarnation; the establishment of the features of universal attachment; the establishment of the methods of teaching, including giving direct and explicit lectures, elucidating meanings respectively, answering questions by asking questions, and keeping silent without saying any word in teaching; and the establishment of conferring prophecies implicitly or explicitly of the achievements the disciples will fulfill in the future, and so forth.

(4-3) The faults are caused by numberless contaminated gates that the Buddha has admonished his disciples.

(4-4) The merits and virtues are caused by numberless pure gates that the Buddha has taught about.

(4-5) The essential meanings as the object of contemplation are the meaning of the reality; the meaning of the realization of the truth; the meaning of teaching and guidance; the meaning of staying away from two extremes; the meaning of the inconceivable things; and the meaning of giving lectures either following teacher's interest or based on audience's interest.

(4-6) The drifting includes three kinds of drifting and four kinds of cause and condition. The three kinds of drifting are arising, duration, and extinction. The four causes and conditions are the cause and condition, the consecutive sequence of thoughts, the conditions that stimulate the mind, and the conditions that reinforce main causes.

(4-7) There are four principles.

(4-7-1) The first is the principle of the arising of various phenomena. This means that as causes and conditions give rise to various phenomena, concepts and language will be created accordingly.

(4-7-2) The second is the principle of operations. This means that after the dharmas arise owing to the combination of causes and conditions, they will accomplish various karmas and continue to bring about more karmas.

(4-7-3) The third is the principle of realization and attainment. This means that the teacher will speak out the statements, then provide evidences or reasons to support the statements, followed by giving examples so that the learners will easily realize the bodhi and attain enlightenment. In this regard, there are two kinds of knowing processes, the pure knowing process and the contaminated knowing process. Five kinds of process are pure: the knowledge formed through direct perception; the knowledge formed indirectly but based on the perceived knowledge; the knowledge formed by analogy; the knowledge formed by perfect realization; and the teaching given with virtuous and pure words. The pure things are valid and useful for forming knowledge. The contaminated process means the process or the path for forming knowledge is not correct, invalid, and misleading, therefore the result is not definite and unreliable. The practitioners should learn the pure ways of forming knowledge, but not the impure ways.

(4-7-4) The fourth is the principle that whether the Thus-Comer appears in the world or not, the dharma is always as it has been.

5) The form of the self-natures of practice and conditions. This indicates the actions and conditions that constitute the factors for enlightenment, such as the

four bases of mindfulness, four correct endeavors, four bases of power, five roots, five powers, and so forth.

6) The form of attaining the effects. This means the merits and virtues of and beyond the world as the effects caused by cultivation and learning. The termination of various kinds of vexations is one of the effects.

7) The form of receiving the teachings. After receiving the correct dharma and also obtaining the superior merits and virtues, the practitioners should further teach what they have learned in order to bring benefits to others.

8) The form of the contaminated dharmas that hinder the pursuit of the correct dharma.

9) The form of the correct dharmas that the practitioners should cultivate diligently.

10) The form of the faultes and mistakes caused by obstacles.

11) The form of the superior benefits. This means the superior merits and virtues caused by the cultivation and learning in accord with correct dharma.

Upon Manjusri Bodhisattva's request to clarify the dharani meanings of sutra, vinaya, and matrka not shared by other paths so that the bodhisattvas were able to insightfully understand the profound secret meanings of the various dharmas that the Thus-Comer taught, the Buddha said that all pure and impure dharmas did not have making and operation; there were no individuals in reincarnation either. As ordinary sentient beings were attached to the thinking that the dharmas and the individuals have different self-natures owing to their hidden roots of vexations and incorrect views, they would misunderstand that the "I" and the associated images were existent. Because of this delusion they would insist that "I see, I hear, I smell, I taste, I touch, I know, I eat, I do, I am contaminated, I am purified, and so forth." As this kind of thinking continues, more and more incorrect views will be generated. If we can understand all dharmas as they really are, our heavy bondages will be terminated permanently and have no more vexations. Then we will stay far away from nonsensical arguments and become extremely pure; we also will rely on nothing and be free from additional efforts. The Buddha said that this was the meaning of dharani that was not shared by other paths.

Manjusri Bodhisattva asked that in filthy lands what things were frequent and what things were rare. The Buddha said that eight things happened often in filthy lands: the practice of other paths; the sentient beings living in suffering; wide gape between different castes; negative actions; violation of laws and lack of respect to precept; rebirth in inferior destinies; pursuit of inferior vehicles; and weak intention for practicing bodhisattva path. Two things happened seldom: Bodhisattvas gathered together to joyfully pursue the bodhi and the Thus-Comer appeared in the world. But in pure lands, the last two things happened often while the first eight things happened rarely.

The Buddha said to Manjusri Bodhisattva that this dharma gate of explaining the profound secret was named the ultimate meaning of the things fulfilled by the Thus-Comer. He encouraged all participants in the assembly should embrace it and practice this profound and secret teaching.

Glossary of Terms

adana: The consciousness that is difficult to know and perceive. It contains the seeds of all dharmas cognized and experienced. When the sentient beings reincarnating in birth and death in the six destinies are reborn, the seeds comprised in mind consciousness mature and reorganize, and two things are ready for holding and receiving: one is the material sense roots and their functions, the other is the name, differentiation, speech, nonsensical arguments, and disposition. This consciousness is also named alaya consciousness. Its other name is mind.

alaya: The eighth consciousness; as the mind functions as the storage of all images caused by one's experiences, it is named alaya.

anuttara-samyak-sambodhi: The unsurpassed, perfect, and universal bodhi attained by the Thus-Comers only. The ultimate goal Buddhist practitioners aspire to achieve.

arhat: The highest stage of voice-hearer cultivation, arhat refers to the one worthy of offerings, who has eliminated all vexations, removed attachment to desires, form, and formlessness, and has been liberated from the bondage of birth and death.

asura: The demigods fond of fighting; one of the eight kinds of heavenly beings or spirits dedicated to the protection of Buddha dharma.

bases of mindfulness, four: Buddhist practitioners are encouraged to be mindful of the four basic contemplations: the body is impure, the feeling is painful, the mind is impermanent, and all dharmas are without selfness. Listed in the thirty-seven aids to enlightenment.

bases of power: The four bases of power that activate, nurture, and fulfill perfect concentration: the powerful motivation and determination to achieve a perfect concentration named aspiration samadhi; concentration practice to rest a wandering mind named mind samadhi; tireless effort to persevere in concentration practice named diligence samadhi; and the practice named contemplation samadhi. Listed in the thirty-seven aids to enlightenment.

Bhagavat: The World-Honored One. One of the ten names of Buddha, meaning he is widely honored and respected in the world because of his unsurpassed merits, virtues, loving-kindness, compassion, knowledge, wisdom, and powers.

bhiksu: The Buddhist monk.

bodhi: Bodhi means wisdom, but not exactly the word commonly understood. The wisdom for the voice-hearers is the voice-hearer bodhi. The wisdom for the self-enlightened ones is the self-enlightenment bodhi. The subtlest and most exquisite knowledge and wisdom that the Thus-Comers realize is the great bodhi, the unsurpassed, perfect, and universal bodhi that the great bodhisattvas aspire to.

bodhisattva, great bodhisattva, bodhisattva mahasattva: The bodhisattva means ones who not only pursue self-awakening but also assists all sentient beings to become awakened. They pursue the unsurpassed, perfect, and universal bodhi in order to bring benefits, peace, and happiness to all sentient beings. Their minds are broad, aspirations widespread, and loving-kindness and compassion for all sentient beings are immeasurable, so they are also named great bodhisattva (bodhisattva mahasattva). The bodhisattva path practice is indispensable for ones to become a Buddha.

bondage of deluded images or the bondage of the forms: The bondage caused by the images or phenomena produced in universal attachment by viewing illusory images as real.

bondage of heavy vexations: The bondage caused by hidden contaminated seeds in mind.

Brahman: One of the four castes in ancient India consisting of the priests in charge of religious rituals and scriptures interpretation. Also used as a general term for Hindu priests.

Buddha dharma: The ultimate meanings of the truths implicitely or explicitly contained in the Buddha's teachings.

conditioned dharma: The transient beings that are caused by integration of causes and conditions and always in change. The conditioned dharmas definitely go through the process of arising, duration, decay, and extinction.

continent of Jambudvipa: One of the four continents located in the south of Mount Sumeru, a land with many jambu trees and jambu gold where live human beings, who are smart and have good memory; they work diligently and learn fast and are privileged to hear and learn the Buddha dharma.

continent of Uttarakuru: Also one of the four continents located in the north of Mount Sumeru, a bright, peaceful, and tranquil land where the sentient beings enjoy a happy life. There are no fights, vicious conduct, or theft.

correct endeavors, four: Working diligently and correctly to discontinue evil things, prevent evil things from occurring, bring virtuous things into existence, and develop and proliferate existing virtuous things. The four correct endeavors are listed in the thirty-seven aids to enlightenment.

Deer Park: The first place where Sakyamuni Buddha turned the dharma wheel right after he realized and attained the unsurpassed, perfect, and universal bodhi. Located in north India with the name Sārnāth nowadays.

dependent origination: One of the natural laws that the Buddha discovered. It means that all existent beings (all dharmas) arise owing to the combination of causes and conditions and extinguish when causes and conditions disintegrate. The world and the existent beings are not created. They are always in change because the causes and conditions and their relations change at all times. In *Samdhinirmocana Sutra,* three forms of nature are established: universal attachment, dependent origination, and perfect realization. Their natures are without selfness in the final analysis.

dharani of hearing and retention: The ability to memorize and retain what one has heard and learned. Dharani is a method of summarizing essential Buddhist teachings; it helps Buddhist practitioners repeat, memorize, uphold, and master what they learn, teach, and practice.

dharma: This is a multi-meaning term. (1) It indicates the ultimate meaning of the truths taught by the Buddha. (2) It means the realty of all dharmas and worldly phenomena. (3) It also means the rules and principles of the world. (4) It is used to indicate the way of correct thinking and behavior. (5) It also refers to all kinds of existent beings in the world or the phenomena of the world; so there are the conditioned dharmas and the unconditioned dharmas, the material dharmas and the immaterial dharmas, the contaminated dharmas and the purified dharmas, the dharmas belonging to the birth and death and the dharmas belonging to nirvana, and so forth.

dharma body: The reality of the dharma; the reality of the truth. Only after cultivating and fulfilling various stages of paramita can the bodhisattvas get away and be transformed into the dharma body of Thus-Comer. It is only in the stage of Thus-Comer that samatha and vipasyana can deal with the subtlest hindrances of extremely minute vexations and knowledge. Once these hindrances are permanently terminated, the bodhisattvas will realize and attain all kinds of perfect knowledge and correct views without attachment and hesitation and establish the purest dharma body. What the voice-hearers and self-enlightened ones can achieve is liberation body instead of dharma body. The transformed body and retribution body of Thus-Comer do arise, but his dharma body does not arise. It is inconceivable, without doing and nonsensical argument.

dharma eye: One of the five eyes inferior only to Buddha eye. A pure and perfect vision of the truth without hindrances.

dharma forbearance of nonarising (Anutpattika-dharma-ksanti): Realizing and accepting the truth that all dharmas are without self-natures and reside in a state of nonarising and nonextinction.

dharma gate: The approaches, ways, and methods by which sentient beings learn the correct dharma, get to know the world, practice the Buddha's teachings, and realize and attain the unsurpassed enlightenment.

dharma nature: The inherently pure, changeless, and equal nature that resides in all existent beings. It is not exactly the dharmas while not apart from the dharmas.

dharma realm: The realm of all existent beings.

eight stages of meditation: In the realm of form, there are the first, second, third, and fourth meditations. In the realm of formlessness, there are the concentration of boundless emptiness, concentration of boundless consciousness, concentration of nothingness, and concentration of nonthinking and not nonthinking.

eighteen realms: The interaction between the six inner spheres (eye, ear, nose, tongue, body, and conscious spheres) and the six outer spheres (sight, sound, smell, taste, touch, and mental-image spheres) causes the six consciousness realms: the eye consciousness, ear consciousness, nose consciousness, tongue consciousness, body consciousness, and conscious consciousness realms. So there are eighteen realms in total in perception process.

emptiness, various kinds of: In *Great Prajna Paramita Sutra,* the Buddha taught about how one can look at emptiness from twenty perspectives. They are internal emptiness (emptiness of eye, ear, nose, tongue, body, and conscious spheres), external emptiness (emptiness of the sight, sound, smell, taste, touch, and mental-image spheres), internal-external emptiness (interaction between the inner and outer spheres), emptiness of emptiness, emptiness of space, emptiness of ultimate truth, emptiness of conditioned phenomena, emptiness of unconditioned reality, emptiness in the final analysis, emptiness of nontemporality, emptiness of deconstruction, emptiness of changelessness, emptiness of original nature, emptiness of particular characteristics, emptiness of common characteristics, emptiness of all dharmas, emptiness of nonattainment, emptiness of selflessness, emptiness of self-nature, and emptiness of selfless self-nature.

factors for enlightenment: There are seven factors for enlightenment: mindfulness, intelligent decision, diligence, joy, ease and freedom, concentration, and equanimity. There are also thirty-seven aids to enlightenment: four bases of mindfulness, four correct endeavors, four bases of power, five roots, five powers, and seven factors for enlightenment.

five coverings: The five mental and moral hindrances that hinder wisdom and bring about vexations; they are desire, hatred and anger, dullness and sleepiness, restless mind and remorse, and doubt.

five powers: The powers caused by belief, diligence, mindfulness, concentration, and wisdom for the great bodhisattvas. Listed in the thirty-seven aids to enlightenment.

five roots: The five flawless roots that contribute to the development of one's abilities in the pursuit of the great bodhi: the roots of faith, diligence, mindfulness, concentration, and wisdom. Also listed in thirty-seven aids to enlightenment.

form: Multiple meanings implied by the term. It refers to the phenomena of the dharmas, the existent beings, the particular characteristics of individual dharmas, or the common traits of dharmas.

four continents: The cosmology of ancient India suggested four continents surrounded by Mount Sumeru and standing in a salty ocean between seven golden mountains and a great circular iron enclosure: the continents of Purvavideha, Jambudvipa, Aparagodaniya, and Uttarakuru.

four kinds of fearlessness: The fearlessness possessed by the Buddhas, not shared by voice-hearers, self-enlightened ones, bodhisattvas, and other sentient beings. The Buddha was fearless to declare publicly that he was fully enlightened; his flaws and vexations had been completely eliminated; his teachings could remove obstacles in pursuing the truth; and his teachings could help learners cease sufferings, even in front of the sramanas, Brahmans, and so forth who were challenging and arguing against him.

four kinds of food: the food for physical body, for sensation, for thinking, and for consciousness.

four noble truths: The four principles that the Buddha frequently taught his disciples to contemplate and realize: suffering, the cause of suffering, the cessation of suffering, and the path for the cessation of suffering.

four paramitas: The Buddha taught the four paramitas to assist bodhisattvas in their cultivation of the six paramitas: expedient skillfulness paramita, aspiration paramita, power paramita, and intelligence paramita.

gandharva: One of the eight kinds of heavenly beings or spirits dedicated to the protection of Buddha dharma; the perfume-eating spirits of music.

Ganges River: The Ganges River in India has been long relied upon by inhabitants for multiple purposes, including agriculture, transportation, drinking water, bathing, and religious rituals.

garuda: The golden-winged birds; one of the eight kinds of heavenly beings or spirits who offer to protect the Buddha dharma.

ghee: ghrta, clarified semifluid butter.

heavy bondages: The power and impact of hidden vexations, that functions as one's stubborn negative disposition.

hidden seeds of vexations: The basic vexations that hide in consciousness since the time unknown; they are subtle and always stay along with the unenlightened ones. Six basic vexations are greed, anger and hatred, ignorance, arrogance, incorrect views, and skepticism. There are five kinds of incorrect views: the thought that self is permanent and real; attachment to extreme points of views, insisting that human life is permanent or one's life discontinues after death; argument against the law of cause and effect; mistaking incorrect views for correct ones; and the belief that some invalid and unreasonable "precepts" or practices will lead one to liberation and enlightenment.

immeasurable minds: Great loving-kindness, great compassion, great joy, and great equanimity are immeasurable because they are unconditioned giving without requesting anything in return; the minds that the great bodhisattvas should learn to embrace.

inferior destinies of rebirth, the negative destinies: Individuals in reincarnation with less merits and virtues but more negative karmas will be reborn in the hells, the realm of animals, or the realm of hungry ghosts; the three inferior or negative realms in rebirth.

kalpa: The period in which the world arises, stays, decays, and extinguishes is named a kalpa. It usually represents an uncountable long period of time. According to Buddhist texts, the present eon is named the Kalpa of the Sages when many Buddhas and bodhisattvas appear; the past eon is the Kalpa of Dignity and the one to come in the future is the Kalpa of Stellar.

karma: The influences of actions that bring about pleasant, painful, or neutral effects.

kimnara: Heavenly singers and dancers who are human-like nonhumans; one of the eight kinds of heavenly beings or spirits dedicated to the protection of Buddha dharma.

koti nayuta: A quantity too large to be calculated or imagined. On the other hand, an extremely small quantity is expressed in Buddhist texts like this: less than one hundredth, one thousandth, one hundred thousandth, one kotith, one hundred kotith, one thousand kotith, one hundred thousand kotith, one nayutath, one hundred nayutath, one thousand nayutath, one hundred thousand nayutath, one hundred thousand koti nayutath, and so forth, and too little to be counted, reckoned, measured, and demonstrated; or as little as one upanisadam-api.

ksana: A very short time.

Ksatriya: The second highest and powerful of the four castes in ancient India; it consists of kings and warriors.

large threefold thousand-world: One large threefold thousand-world comprises one thousand medium thousand-worlds; one medium thousand-world (medium chilocosm) comprises one thousand small thousand-worlds; while one small thousand-world (small chilocosm) comprises one thousand smaller worlds, in which mountains, heavens, oceans, and continents are found. A way of expressing a huge multiple universe or world, originated in ancient India and has been adopted by Buddhist texts.

large vehicle or great vehicle: The three vehicles of the voice-hearer, self-enlightened one, and bodhisattva are mentioned in Buddhist texts. The first two vehicles are much smaller than the third one. The large vehicle is capable of ferrying numberless sentient beings across the river to the other shore of permanent peaceful nirvana. The first two vehicles focus on self-liberation, while the bodhisattva-path practitioners vow to liberate all sentient beings.

liberation body: This means the reality of liberation. When the voice-hearers and self-enlightened ones become liberated from all vexations, they are named attaining liberation body. In terms of liberation body, the voice-hearers and self-enlightened ones are equivalent to Thus-Comers, but in terms of dharma body they are much inferior to Thus-Comers because their merits and virtues are much less by numberless times.

mahoraga: Snake spirits; one of the eight kinds of heavenly beings or spirits dedicated to the protection of Buddha dharma.

matrka: A Sanskrit word which means the treatise.

medium thousand-world: Please see large threefold thousand-world.

naga: Heavenly dragons, one of the eight kinds of heavenly beings or spirits dedicated to the protection of Buddha dharma.

nirvana: A state of perfect liberation and tranquility achieved by ones who are free from vexations and bondages, dwell in nonaction and nondifferentiation, and transcend arising and extinction. A state that signifies the fulfillment of perfect enlightenment.

nirvana with remainder: In this nirvana, ones' karmic effects are mature or not mature, and their vexations have been eliminated permanently. They still have physical bodies and feelings, but because their feelings are purified they are free from heavy bondages.

nirvana without remainder: A state of nirvana in which physical body does not exist, karmic effects are cleared, and all vexations are eliminated permanently. A complete freedom from all kinds of bondages.

noble eightfold path: The noble eightfold path consists of the right view, right thinking, right speech, right action, right livelihood, right diligence, right mindfulness, and the right concentration. This is the path for the cessation of suffering.

perfect realization: Fully realizing that all dharmas are dependently originated and their natures are without self-natures, arising, and extinction. This is the perfect realization of the reality of all dharmas.

prajna: A Sanskrit which means exquisite and superior wisdom of the world and beyond the world. The basis of the six paramitas. All virtuous dharmas are absorbed in prajna. It is because of the prajna paramita that the bodhisattvas are able to fulfill the cultivation of all virtuous dharmas and become the Buddha. Based on the realization of the ultimate meanings of all dharmas and knowing that they are empty, selfless, nonexistent, and without attachment and attainment, prajna teaches bodhisattva-path aspirants the way for expedient skillfulness.

realness: The essence of existent beings and a paradigm of the forms and rules of all operations in the world. The reality that resides in all dharmas, spheres, and realms evenly. It is also named dharma realm, dharma nature, and the nature of equality. It comprises and transcends the beings in space and time. It changes and arises, but in the final analysis it does not change or arise at all, and it is therefore named the nature of changelessness and the nature of nonarising. It is as vast as boundless space and spreads and fills all, so it is named the realm of empty space. It is the basis of peace and tranquility on which all beings rely and all sentient beings rest; therefore it is also named dharma concentration or dharma dwelling. It is beyond human logical understanding and imagination, so it is the realm of the inconceivable.

samadhi: A calm and concentrative state of mind in which positive outcomes are produced as a result of tranquil concentration (samatha) and insightful investigation (vipasyana). A correct and equal mindfulness.

samadhi with contemplation and investigation: When absorbing and examining the images in samatha and vipasyana and acquiring a rough and not so refined indication of perception, the bodhisattvas are undertaking the samadhi with contemplation and investigation. In addition, if the bodhisattvas search and investigate with an intention, they are also doing the samadhi with contemplation and investigation.

samadhi with investigation only: Although the bodhisattvas practice samatha and vipasyaba and do not have a rough and obvious indication of perception, they do have a subtle and brilliant light in perception. This is the samadhi with investigation only. If there is an investigation undertaken in samatha and vipasyana, they are also in the samadhi with investigation only.

samadhi without contemplation and investigation: When practicing samatha and vipasyana, the bodhisattvas do not have any intention to think, percept, and observe; they are undertaking the samadhi without contemplation and investigation. If they follow the general approach to practice samatha and vipasyana, they are also in the samadhi without contemplation and investigation.

samapatti: Staying in a deeper mental and physical state of tranquility with longer duration than samadhi.

samatha: Mind concentrates and dwells in calmness and serenity.

self-enlightened one (pratyekabuddha): Some learners are very shy or fond of living alone, so they choose to learn and practice by themselves and become enlightened. Some have to do so because the Buddha dharma is not available. This also means that one has become enlightened by realizing the twelve chains of arising based on the law of dependent origination. Both voice-hearers (sravaka) and self-enlightened one incline to practice and cultivate in order to liberate themselves instead of delivering all sentient beings.

six inner spheres: The eye, ear, nose, tongue, body, and conscious spheres are the perceiving subjects.

six outer spheres: The sight, sound, smell, taste, touch, and mental-image spheres are the perceived objects.

six paramitas: giving paramita, pure-precept paramita, forbearance paramita, diligence paramita, meditation paramita, and prajna paramita. These are the core courses for learning to become a bodhisattva. Paramita means perfection; the cultivation that reaches perfection at uppermost level is paramita. It also means ferrying oneself and many others from this shore of vexations and suffering to the other shore of liberation, peace, and tranquility. For more elaborated description of these six paramitas, please read chapter 7 of this sutra.

small thousand-world: Please see large threefold thousand-world.

ten abilities: The Buddha's ten abilities not shared by other sentient beings are: the ability to know the laws of cause and effect and so forth, and to tell the right from the wrong; the ability to know the karmic causes and effects of the sentient beings in the past, future, and present as they really are; the ability to know the characteristics of numberless realms of the sentient beings as they really are; the ability to know the beliefs and understandings of all sentient beings as they really are; the ability to know the strengths and weaknesses of all sentient beings as they really are; the ability to know the characteristics of the five universal functions concomitant at all times with perceptive activities of the sentient beings as they really are; the ability to know the samadhi and samapatti of meditations and the conditions of liberation that are pure or impure of the sentient beings as they really are; the ability to know the previous lives of the sentient beings as they really are; the ability to know the birth and death of the sentient beings as they really are; and the ability to know that whether one's flaws and defilements have been completely removed or not as they really are.

ten paramitas: The six paramitas and the four paramitas make the ten paramitas. Please see six paramitas and four paramitas.

ten stages of bodhisattva cultivation: The stages of ecstasy, freedom from defilements, emitting light, flaming wisdom, being extremely difficult to be surpassed, realness manifestation, going far away, the unmovable, expedient wisdom, and dharma cloud. Please see Chapter 7 of this sutra for the elaboration of these ten stages.

thirty-two perfect major marks: The perfect features of body and demeanors of the Buddha as the results of his unsurpassed wisdom, power, virtues, and merits. They are:

1. The Buddha's feet have flat and full soles, which are exquisite and are as firm and stable as the bottom of a solid makeup case; wherever he walks, his soles touch the ground evenly and completely.

2. There are perfect thousand-spoke wheel signs on his soles.

3. His hands and feet are flexible and soft.

4. His fingers and toes are webbed, resembling those of the wild goose king.

5. He has slender and round fingers and toes.

6. He has wide, long, and perfect heels, matching the insteps very well.

7. He has slender, high, and full insteps, matching the heels very well.

8. He has slender and round shins in good proportion, like that of the deer king.

9. His slender and long arms extend past the knees like the trunk of the elephant king.

10. His male sex organ is concealed, resembling that of a dragon, a horse, or the elephant king.

11. There is one hair in each of his pores.

12. All his hair stands straight up in a right-handed rotation.

13. His skin is delicate and moisturized.

14. All his skin is a golden color and is clean and bright.

15. His legs, palms, shoulders, and neck are delicate and full, and the muscles are soft.

16. He has perfect and wonderful shoulders and neck.

17. His shoulder blades and armpits are full and round.

18. His face and manner are perfect, proper, and upright.

19. The shape of his body is slender, wide, solemn, and upright.

20. The span of his arms equals the height of his body; the profile of his body is as perfect as a nyagrodha tree.

21. His upper body, chin, and chest are big and wide, resembling that of the lion king.

22. Bright light always radiates from his face.

23. He has forty neat and white teeth.

24. He has four white canine teeth.

25. He has flavored saliva, swallows smoothly, and always has the most delicious taste when eating.

26. His tongue is long, slender, pure, and broad and can reach the edge of his hair.

27. His voice is as loud and powerful as the heavenly drum. When he recites, his voice is so graceful and far-reaching that all listeners can hear him clearly and evenly. When he speaks, his voice vibrates with resonance.

28. His eyelashes are deep blue and neat, like that of a bull king.

29. His eyes are deep blue and bright.

30. His face is like a full moon, and his eyebrows are like the bows used by the heavenly gods.

31. There are white hairs between his eyebrows.

32. He has a bump on the top of the head.

Thus-Comer (tathagata): The Thus-Comers are the fully developed, perfect ones. They have come in such a natural and spontaneous way; they have come through a stable and peaceful path; but they neither come nor not come. The Thus-Comers know and teach the phenomena of all dharmas as they really are. They insightfully understand realness. They accomplish ultimate nirvana based on the unsurpassed, perfect, and universal bodhi. They have fulfilled all virtuous karmas and eliminated all bad karmas permanently. They have lectured on the fundamental path of liberation and led sentient beings to stay away from negative paths and stay on correct path. So they are named Thus-Comer.

three liberation gates: The liberation gates of emptiness, formlessness, and nonaspiration.

three realms: the realm of desire, the realm of form, and the realm of formlessness.

twelve chains of dependent arising: The Buddha became awakened to the truth of the twelve chains of dependent arising at the moment of attaining the unsurpassed, perfect, and universal bodhi. For ordinary sentient beings, the chains form a circle of reincarnation based on negative karmas, while the enlightened holy ones are able to trace the circle back to the cause of all suffering and untie the chains of life. For the former ones, the flow of the three modes of time is shown as a successive cause-and-effect connection in the change of one's life-form. The core of this life-drifting is consciousness, the alaya, which is viewed as a storage of one's karmas. The twelve chains are: ignorance causes action, action causes consciousness, consciousness causes name and form, name and form cause six sense spheres, six sense spheres cause contact, contact causes reception, reception causes craving, craving causes grasping, grasping causes existence, existence causes birth, and birth causes old age, death, worry, sorrow, misery, and upset. The way back from birth and death and many pains thus derived to the cause of all suffering as traced by enlightened practitioners through knowledge and cultivation to remove the first cause will make them liberated from birth and death.

twelve divisions of Buddha's teachings: The Buddha's teachings were given in different styles; they were recorded and compiled under twelve canonical divisions: the texts (sutra), short verses (geya), prophecy (vyakarana), long verses (gatha), self-statement (udana), origins (nidana), similes (avadana), anecdotes (itivrttaka), past lives (jataka), broad teaching (vaipulya), unusual ways (abdhuta-dharma), and discourses (upadesa).

1 sutra: The general name for the recorded texts of the teachings given by the Buddha.

2 geya: A partial repeat of sutra in verse style.

3 vyakarana: The stories that record the Buddha's prophecies about his disciples or followers who will become a Buddha in the future, including when, where, and with what names.

4 gatha: The Buddha's teachings given in verse style.

5 udana: Lectures initiated by the Buddha himself, not upon his disciples' request.

6 nidana: The origin and background of how and why the Buddha's teachings are given.

7 avadana: The similes and the celebrated stories of ancient sages given in Buddha's teachings.

8 itivrttaka: What the Buddha and his disciples did in their past lives, but no exact times and places of the events were indicated.

9 jataka: The stories of the Buddha's compassionate deeds in previous lives when he was still a bodhisattva.

10 vaipulya: The teachings of the ultimate truth with elaborated interpretation and in-depth analysis.

11 adbhuta-dharma: The record of the Buddha and his disciples' mystic and unusual conducts.

12 upadesa: The Buddha's teachings given in discursive way.

twelve spheres: The twelve spheres contain the six inner spheres and six outer spheres. The six inner spheres are the eye, ear, nose, tongue, body, and conscious spheres; these are the six sense roots forming the perceiving subject. The six outer spheres are the sight, sound, smell, taste, touch, and mental-image spheres; they are the perceived objects.

unconditioned dharma: The dharmas that do not arise and extinguish, or stay and decay. They are neither contaminated nor purified. They do not increase or decrease and are without form and action. Their self-natures are no nature.

universal attachment: For the unenlightened ones, the phenomena of the world look so real. Because they do not realize that all dharmas are dependently originated, without selfness, and nonexistent in the final analysis, they mistake changing images for real and become attached to their existence. Vexations and suffering thus are brought about, reincarnation in birth and death are initiated. The universal attachment of ordinary sentient beings to the phenomenal world are caused by the lack of insightful realization and awakening.

unsurpassed, perfect, and universal bodhi: Please see anuttara-samyak-sambodhi.

upanisadam-api: A Sanskrit which means an extremely small quantity. The smallest unit of matter that can be divided.

vinaya: The precepts and behavioral rules for monastics established by the Buddha.

vipasyana: Insightful investigation either by logical reflection, analysis, or intuitive contemplation based on samatha. There are three kinds of vipasyana: the vipasyana with perceived images, the vipasyana of general contemplation, and the vipasyana of specific investigation.

voice-hearer (sravaka): The Buddha's disciples who directly heard teachings from the Buddha. The highest stage in the cultivation of this path mainly with self-liberation intention is arhat; the three stages preceding it are stream-enterer, once-returner, and nonreturner.

Worldly-Honored One: Please see Bhagavat.

yaksa: The flying spirits of the dead; one of the eight kinds of heavenly beings or spirits dedicated to the protection of Buddha dharma.